LETS GO

GO

PUBLISH

LETS GO United States of America!

The Bill of Rights 4 Dummmies

Your first book to read to refresh your knowledge of the rights granted to all Americans.

Read *The Bill of Rights 4 Dummmies* so you understand your rights & your freedoms, so that none of the nerds in government can take them from you!

Learn about your rights and freedoms by reading The Bill of Rights 4 Dummmies! After understanding the Constitution, this is the best thing you can do to understand your role in assuring our great form of government without being snookered by anybody!

This book is the best starter book for anybody, especially those unsure of what America offers in the way of rights, duties, and powers. This book is to help you be better prepared to react to the over-reach of corrupt politicians at the highest levels of government. Know your rights!

Without the knowledge that you can gain easily in this book, for example, you might think that your representatives in Congress holds all the cards, and that mum is the word. You may think that you can speak freely only in the free speech zones of American universities. That is crap and you should know it!

Today more than ever with the government attempting to control the people, it is a great thing for Americans to know that we run the government and the government does not run us. Americans need to know our rights and the protections built into the basic framework of our government formed by the US Constitution and the Bill of Rights. Why did we wait so long?

Just because powerful people choose to ignore our rights and freedoms does not mean we must endure tyranny. The first step of course is to understand the most basic written precepts in the Constitution. Reading this book is a must.

LETS GO PUBLISH

BRIAN W. KELLY

Copyright © 2014, Brian W. Kelly
The Bill of Rights 4 Dummmies!

Editor: Brian P. Kelly
Author Brian W. Kelly

Referenced Material : *Standard Disclaimer: The information in this book has been obtained through personal and third party observations, interviews, and copious research. Where unique information has been provided or extracted from other sources, those sources are acknowledged within the text of the book itself or at the end of the chapter in the Sources Section. Thus, there are no formal footnotes nor is there a bibliography section. Any picture that does not have a source was taken from various sites on the Internet with no credit attached. If resource owners would like credit in the next printing, please email publisher.*

Published by: ....LETS GO PUBLISH!
Editor ....Brian P. Kelly
Email: ....info@letsgopublish.com
Web site ....www.letsgopublish.com

Library of Congress Copyright Information Pending
Book Cover Design by Michele Thomas, Associate Editor—Brian P. Kelly

ISBN Information: The International Standard Book Number (ISBN) is a unique machine-readable identification number, which marks any book unmistakably. The ISBN is the clear standard in the book industry. 159 countries and territories are officially ISBN members. The Official ISBN For this book is on the outside cover:

ISBN: **978-0-9899957-7-1**

The price for this work is:								**$12.88 USD**	
10	9	8	7	6	5	4	3	2	1
Release Date:								August	
2014									

Dedication

To the entire Kelly Family.
(My father's side of the family)

They have all stood there with me and I with them, as we seek the truth and continue our fight for our freedoms.

The gentlemen Kellys on this list fought in World War II or the Korean War. We thank them deeply for their service.

Uncle Mart, Uncle Ed, Aunt Marie, Aunt Catherine, Aunt Helen, Uncle Pat, Uncle Mike, Uncle Phil, Uncle Joe, and Uncle Johnnie

Acknowledgments

In every book that I write or edit, I publicly acknowledged all of the help that I have received from many sources. Some of these wonderful people are still on earth and others have made their way to heaven.

I would like to thank many people for helping me in this effort. I appreciate all the help that I received in putting this book together, along with the 66 other books from the past.

My printed acknowledgments were once so large that book readers needed to navigate too many pages to get to page one of the text. To permit me more flexibility, I put my acknowledgment list online at www.letsgopublish.com. The list of acknowledgments continues to grow. Believe it or not, it once cost about a dollar more to print each book.

Thank you all on the big list in the sky and God bless you all for your help.

Please check out www.letsgopublish.com to read the latest version of my heartfelt acknowledgments updated for this book. Thank you all!

In this book, I received some extra special help from many avid Notre Dame supporters including Bruce Ikeda, Dennis Grimes, Gerry Rodski, Wily Ky Eyely, Angel Irene McKeown Kelly, Angel Edward Joseph Kelly Sr., Angel Edward Joseph Kelly Jr., Ann Flannery, Angel James Flannery Sr., Mary Daniels, Bill Daniels, Robert Gary Daniels, Angel Sarah Janice Daniels, Angel Punkie Daniels, Joe Kelly, Diane Kelly, Brian P. Kelly, Mike P. Kelly, Katie P. Kelly, Ben Kelly, and Budmund (Buddy) Arthur Kelly.

Preface

Do we Americans deserve any rights? If you listen to the popular press and to the liberal communist progressives that are overwhelming our government today, you will conclude they think the answer is "no." There are more of us than them so please do not get hoodwinked believing any of their bull...

This one sentence speech might fly in Central America but it is not going to fly once real Americans understand what they are giving up: "Why should Americans have lives that are nice when the rest of the world is suffering?

Why is the US press and the bulk of government workers so anti-American? Maybe they should take up residence someplace else and torment another group of people.

Early Americans fought for our rights and later Americans fought to preserve them. Communists were never interested in protecting our rights in the beginning, the middle, and surely not now when many non-thinking Americans are prepared to hand our country over to them.

So, what rhetoric would you expect from those that espouse an ideology that says government should take from you so that Joe Bloe down the street should never have to worry about working? Joe Bloe will never have any rights other than the short term right to not work for his meager welfare payments. Since neither Communism nor communism has ever worked in any country, you and I know that life won't always be sweet for Joe Bloe and Mary Bloe. However, neither Joe nor Mary know it and they would not believe you if you read the history of the world to them 100 or more times.

American rights are not a gift. They were not donated to Americans by anybody. Many Americans fought and many died for independence from the tyranny of England as well as in World Wars and other wars. America was always on the side of right.

Once our own independence, freedoms, and liberties were gained from the bloodshed, the objective always was to keep the rest of the world safe and permit the whole world to live as well as it could. America and Americans have helped our neighbors across the world.

The graves of our sons and fathers with tombstones stretched across the world are vivid proof of our kindness as a country and our desire to help all the people of the world to become or to remain free. Don't let the blame America first crowd; talk down America while you are in the room. America and Americans deserve better.

Americans should not have to apologize to anybody. We should have no guilt. Yet, our bought and paid for corrupt press and our current government would love to ram tyranny down our throats by telling us we are bad people. Please don't buy any of it. We are not bad people. We are exceptional people. Nobody has ever done in the existence of recorded history as much as America and Americans have done for our fellow man.

Wait until a Democrat, a progressive, a Marxist, or a communist says something good about America, and you will be waiting a lifetime. Think about that while you consider that big government is good for the people. Think again, please.

It has been 225 plus years since the United States, our country, achieved independence. Along with independence, we earned freedom and liberty. Nobody has a right to demean US for that and nobody can take it away.

Ironically, there are some in America who espouse the liberal progressive Marxist ideology that are ready to blame America first for everything. Ironically, here we are, 225 plus years after the Constitution and we cannot get these people to agree that freedom is a good thing. As far as I am concerned it is OK if they all left town and went to their favorite suppressed country to practice their ideology. They hurt America every day.

Though all is not perfect in America, the principles of the Constitution and the Bill of Rights are so sound and so powerful that even a knave politician cannot bring us under. The big concern of course is that if we don't smarten up, things will get a lot worse. I suspect that is why you are reading this book.

Our ailments are large and growing. Taxes are too high, elected officials are out of touch, government is too big, spending is out of control; the new healthcare program is a train wreck, the federal government is incompetent, the people have no voice in government, too many people are too lazy to hold government accountable, too many are on the take, and worse than that, the list of ailments is growing, not shortening.

Things are happening that are lawless. In 2014, for example, the leader of the free world, without the required permissions of the US Congress, traded five terrorists for a POW who had deserted his unit in Afghanistan. The father praised Allah and that too was difficult to understand considering the negotiations with the Taliban had been fruitless for years.

Meanwhile a former marine, a documented hero, while I write this word, is rotting in a Mexican jail. Why? Because the leader of the free world will not pick up his phone and his pen and demand that he be released. Instead after a few more months of punishment for him being in the military, the President will have an epiphany and emerge in a political ceremony claiming he did not know about the Marine's plight. Then, he will take credit for his release. We'll see. I wish I trusted more but it is tough to trust a liar.

Your intention no doubt in learning about the structure of America and its most fundamental laws in choosing to read this book is to help you understand why all this is happening. Thank you. That is why Brian W. wrote this book. I am betting that more sooner than later, you will better understand our great country and our great form of government—at least before the bad guys take it away.

This book is the best starter book for anybody wanting to refresh their knowledge or learn about the government of the United States of America and to be better prepared to react to the over-reach of today's corrupt politicians at the highest levels of government. Without the knowledge that you can gain easily in this book, for example, you might not understand your rights.

This might cause you to unknowingly be convinced by socialist progressives in the government that you have no rights, and you have no freedoms, and any of your permissions come from the government itself.

If you have been paying attention to what is going on in America today, you know we are in trouble. We have a busted economy, high unemployment, no jobs, and our basic rights to freedoms such as speech, religion, the press, and our right-to-bear-arms are being impinged upon. The Founders saw it as a civic duty for Americans to *pay attention* to our government so that we can avoid being chumps and being snookered by crooked politicians.

There are more issues than just those noted above, and we better fix them quickly while we still have a Constitution and a Bill of Rights upon which to lean.

We are on the same side in this battle for the Constitution, the Bill of Rights, and for the survival of America. Together we can all help. We first must understand what is going on and we then must understand our rights as delivered in the Declaration of Independence, The Constitution, and the Bill of Rights.

My concern is that when we all wake up from our deep fog, there may be no Bill of Rights or Constitution left for our progeny. We will have blown it for sure if that is permitted to happen.

In this book, Kelly unabashedly recommends that we stop trusting government since it is clearly not working for our best interests. The sooner we can understand the threat from the Left, the sooner we can move on to solving the problem for our values, our country, and our freedom.

The smarter we are, the more chance we have for success. Understanding America's founding and the founding documents, especially the Constitution and The Bill of Rights, is a sure way to become an American forever. I know you love America as I do.

Your author continually monitors what is happening to our government and he has written extensively on the major problems our country faces. Brian W. Kelly is one of America's most outspoken and eloquent conservative spokesmen. He is the author of America 4 Dummmies, The Constitution 4 Dummmies, Sol Bloom's Epoch Story of the Constititution, No Amnesty! No Way!, Saving America, Taxation Without Representation, Obama's Seven Deadly Sins, Kill the EPA!, Jobs! Jobs! Jobs!. The Federalist Papers by the Framers, and many other patriotic books. All books are available at www.bookhawkers.com.

Like many Americans, Brian W. is fed up with stifling socialist progressive Marxists in the top seats in Washington. They place the needs of everybody else in front of the needs of Americans. Like many Americans, Kelly is shocked at how brazen the administration is today in ignoring our Constitution and our Bill of Rights! This must be stopped.

Brian W. Kelly has read the founding documents, the underlying intelligence reports, and he has researched and written about such topics for years. Brian has written fifty-five books and hundreds of patriotic articles. He is deeply concerned about how intolerable the results of poor government policy can be within our neighborhoods and our lives. His comprehensible and sane recommendations in this book are explained in detail within the covers of this soon-to-be classic edition.

The Bill of Rights 4 Dummmies is a title to get your attention for sure. I hope we got your attention. In addition to a review of the founding history, your author has included a major civics lesson in this book to bring you up to date on the national scene. Additionally, he has included copies of the founding documents so that you can read them directly in this book, rather than on the Internet.

You are going to love this book, designed by an American for Americans. Few books are must-read but *The Bill of Rights 4 Dummmies* will quickly be at the top of America's most read list.

Sincerely,

Brian P. Kelly, Editor

Table of Contents

About the Author

Brian W. Kelly retired as an Assistant Professor in the Business Information Technology (BIT) program at Marywood University, where he also served as the IBM i and midrange systems technical advisor to the IT faculty. Kelly has designed, developed, and taught many college and professional courses. He is also a contributing technical editor to a number of IT industry magazines, including "The Four Hundred" and "Four Hundred Guru" published by IT Jungle. On the Patriotic side, you once could find a patriotic Kelly article at www.conservativeactionalerts.com. This site no longer functions but the articles are still hosted at www.brianwkelly.com

Kelly is a former IBM Senior Systems Engineer and he has been a candidate for US Congress and the US Senate from Pennsylvania. He has an active information technology consultancy. He is the author of 67 books and numerous articles. Kelly is a frequent speaker at National Conferences, and other technical conferences. Ask him to speak at your next TEA Party rally! You might be surprised!

Over the past twenty years, Brian Kelly has become one of America's most outspoken and eloquent conservative protagonists. Besides The Bill of Rights 4 Dummmies, America 4 Dummmies, and The Constitution 4 Dummmies, Kelly is also the author of No Amnesty! No Way!, Taxation Without Representation, and many other patriotic books. Books are available at www.bookhawkers.com

Endorsed by the Independence Hall Tea Party in 2010, Kelly, a Democrat, ran for Congress against a 13-term Democrat and, took no campaign contributions, spent enough to buy signs and T-shirts, and as a virtual unknown, he captured 17% of the vote— www.briankellyforcongress.com. Kelly then supported Republican challenger Lou Barletta, a conservative leader on immigration policy, and helped him win a resounding victory in the general election.

Chapter 1 Americans Are Mad as Hell about Our Dwindling Rights!

Mad as hell with no rights!

Hollywood in 2014 is fairly solidly behind all Democratic leaders, both in Congress and in the White House. One might conclude that it does not matter in which neighborhood you live, as long as you swing with the lefties; you can be assured of love and respect from the Hollywood elite—even if they do not know you from Adam. FYI, Hollywood does not care about your rights or mine—just theirs!

By the way, it does not matter if you are a politician or a reprobate, or you happen to simply be a member of the low information crowd. If you vote on the left side of the ballot box with the communists, and the redistributionists, you are welcomed with open arms in the town with the name on the hill. Welcome to Hollywood!

Today Americans on the left and the right are being asked to give up their rights so that others, who are jealous of those rights, can be made happy. Today's government leaders in all parties lean left and love to call themselves progressives. Being a progressive today gives an American rights that the founders never dreamed anybody would need.

For example, a progressive has the right to lie up a storm and he or she can always expect the mainstream media to swear that their word is the Gospel. A progressive can always say they did not take the cookie from the jar, even if their finger prints are all over the jar, and Lieutenant Columbo is saying: "Oh, oh, one more thing, before I forget..."

Moreover—and this is even better, the person who accuses a progressive of snatching the cookie is the most likely to take the rap—even if the progressive has as many as four full, though somewhat saliva melted chocolate chips and as many as seven independent chocolate stains on their lips. The point is that liberal progressives seem to have more rights than reality can imagine—including the rights to lie, cheat, and steal with impunity, especially if the real victim is a conservative.

Presidents and Congressmen in the decade between 2010 and 2020 get to lie for free and the media enjoys covering for them. The low information crowd (LIC) has lost the ability to discern a lie from the truth. Therefore lies do not affect the likeability or the electability of a politician. By the way, LICs cannot even discern the meaning of the word discern. That's why our country is in trouble. LICs brag about their lack of knowledge on most subjects when interviewed on the Late Night TV celebrity road trips. But their dummmness is not really funny.

We live in a world in which real scandals are mocked as fake scandals and late night TV hosts are the only ones who can tell a real scandal from a "fake scandal."

Some of the scandals about which we have learned from government and media sources are in the fake variety according to official government sources.

These include "non-scandals" such as Benghazi, Syria, NSA, IRS, Taliban Prisoner Exchange, etc. The country's chief executive, for example, knows most of these are fake because as he has said repeatedly, he had just learned about the problem on his way to a fundraiser. He read about NSA, the IRS, Benghazi and other fake scandals under the Fake Scandals section of the daily newspaper.

Ironically, just past the sixth year mark in his second term, "W" Bush had engaged in just over 200 fund-raisers while Obama has been engaged in well over 400 fund raisers in the same time period. George Bush played about 25 rounds of golf and Obama played about 200 rounds of golf in the same time period.

Bush thinks because of the pressure in the bubble, the folks should not criticize all the Golf that Obama plays. With 400 fund raisers, not including the *to and from* flight days, and 200 golf dates, there sure is not much time for governing. Many conservatives are hoping the President goes on more fundraisers and plays more golf. It seems to be good for the country.

Even Stephen Colbert, who has recently become the "darling of the far lefties," reaching for some personal dignity found that even he could not deny the flagrant corruption of President Obama's VA Hospital / Veterans' Care system. Too bad the President was unaware of that one.

Maybe Colbert will be fired soon because Hollywood does not like the truth. Howard Beale, who you will meet soon, got fired. Jay Leno got fired. Lou Dobbs got fired. Will Colbert get fired? The truth is not a popular theme in Hollywood and it is less popular in TV-Land!.

The one-time Comedy Central host (now Late Show Host) Colbert acknowledged the importance of the VA scandal while simultaneously mocking it a few days prior to Memorial Day on his May 22 Colbert Report. Complete with a balloon drop, it was a classic Colbert with an over-the-top fake celebration of the "real" VA scandal.

But, the fun it poked at conservatives for having been fixated on the "fake" scandals, got lost in the reality of so many great Americans getting hosed by the Government in the real world, according to Colbert, VA scandal.

Whether you believe all of this administration's "fake scandals" are trumped up publicity events by those nasty Republicans, or not, one thing we do know in the line of inconvenient truths is that four people died in Benghazi when none should have died.

Another thing we know is that red lines soon turn pink if not crossed in time to politically help a president. We know that NSA spying always helps the chances of lefties getting elected. Additionally, we know that IRS corruption always helps the chances of lefties getting elected.

In the most obvious category, we know that depleting the nasty prisoner contingent in Guantanamo Bay (Gitmo) always helps the lefties love their leaders even more and who could ask for anything more? Oh, and by the way, something the lefties like to suggest: "Deserters are people too!" Sorry, I almost forgot to mention that one.

In the new gumment—don't you just love my buddy Jim Faller's newly coined word for government —gumment executives, especially presidents, are now immune from the consequences of skipping daily security briefings.

Moreover, a sure way to throw off the LICs so they lean left is not only to blame Bush for everything imaginable but also to suggest that if you think you are upset about what happened; think about how bad the President feels, having just learned about the "problem." When the leader of the free world learned about any of these major issues in the daily paper, the leader was even more upset than the people. He was mad as hell for sure. He had a right to be!

I do not want to be disrespectful to the institution of the US Presidency. Neither does Charles Krauthammer, a paraplegic who still has the sharpest mind on the planet. These are his words:

How can Obama be so surprised so often?

"It's as if he wandered into the White House on a tour and discovered he's President."
- Charles Krauthammer

LessGovMoreFun.Com

Every now and then, a Hollywood guy goes off the farm or as some say: *"off the reservation,"* and insists on telling a new truth, which most often makes the old lies look like they too are true. It is a great trick and it can deliver a lot of laughs in Hollywood if delivered properly. Moreover, it can make the lefties seem smart at times.

Some elitists may say that only those Americans who are really stupid are unaware that today's President is mad as hell that such things as the fake scandals can happen. They also suggest that this President gets even madder when he has to read the newspaper to find out about the fake scandals. They know he is working hard to make everything better—working really hard because he loves America deeply though his love of America is shared equally with the First Lady.

Our country's CEO, the leader of the free world, who would have gladly served in Vietnam but was too young (just six years old) and at the time, unfortunately, he was living in a Muslim Country (Indonesia), which would not release him for duty anyway.

At the time, being six years old was not the major reason for the President to not have been able to serve America in Vietnam. As an aside, the largest Muslim population in any country is in Indonesia, but of course that does not cast any aspersions upon anybody mentioned in this chapter.

The Leader of the free world wants all Americans to believe that he has the best intentions and regardless of the crisis du jour, or as the Republicans would call it, the "scandal du jour," he will use his patented formula, which he developed from his substantial personal experience in the free world. "He will study the situation and take the most appropriate action—but only when the time is right." Who could want for more?

Just as the leader of the Free World, our president, I too am mad as hell about a government that permits America to be demeaned by either incompetence or intentional efforts towards its destruction.

However, this is not the purpose of this book, though government lies do limit all of our rights that are enumerated in the Bill of Rights and the Constitution. It is however, the underlying truth about why I wrote the book. Would it not be nice if we all told the truth—especially if the truth tellers were high ranking government officials?

In case you missed it in one of my recent books, *America for Dummmies!;* we're going to start out exactly the same way in this book, but we will quickly get on to the meat of the US Bill of Rights, the precious adjunct to the most wonderful document other than the Bible itself—written by the hand of God. I speak of course of the US Constitution.

In essence, Americans are upset today because our Constitution is under attack, and the Constitution is the framework that enables our Bill of Rights. As most historians, and those who studied sixth grade history once knew, the Bill of Rights enumerates specific rights for Americans.

The Constitution which is the big boss over the Bill of Rights says that any rights not so enumerated in the Constitution belong to the people, not the government. Today's government officials as we all know, unfortunately seem to see it differently. By the time you finish this book, you will have no sympathy for them.

The Constitution—the law of the land—the basis for the Bill of Rights, which you are about to explore; is unlawfully being bypassed by opportunists today in government. That makes a lot of US "Mad as Hell!" Howard Beale in the paragraphs below represents all frustrated Americans. His story, though unrelated to the theme in the book, really captures the mood and the emotions of America today regarding a government gone wild! *Wild* in this case is a synonym for *"bad."*

You may not remember because you are probably not old enough; though many of you have enough life mileage to have seen the movie long after its debut in 1976.

So, if you have some life baggage, and you have some time on your bones, you may remember back in November, 1976 when Howard Beale, as played by Peter Finch, the long-time anchor in the "Hollywood" movie "Network News," gets the bad news that eventually causes him to utter one of the most famous movie lines of all time.

Beale gets fired and is given two weeks. The long-time anchor has a very poor reaction to this news and he cannot control himself during the next news broadcast. You get the feeling that he saw his perceived "rights" being violated.

He promises to commit suicide on the air. The company immediately fires him—no second chances for a repeat performance. Beale is devastated and remorseful. He begs for the opportunity to say good-by to his fans with dignity, and he is given his last opportunity ever for air time so that he can say his good-by's to his public and also apologize. He gets his chance

Yet, once on the air, the one-time network news anchorman is overwhelmed by his continuing circumstance. He goes into another diatribe starting off with a rant claiming that "Life is bullshit." He is so passionate that his ratings spike as he persuades his viewers to shout out of their windows: "I'm as mad as hell, and I'm not going to take this anymore!" That is the line heard 'round the world.

Well, my fellow Americans, I bet you saw this coming, and I am going to deliver it as passionately in words as I can: "I am mad as hell, and I am not going to take this anymore." I bet you are too. Let me remind you. Besides one rights violation by government after another, there are the usual issues, but these issues are far worse today than ever before in our country's history.

Chapter 2   Mad as Hell, With Good Reasons!

The government has created a train wreck... everywhere!

Taxes are too high, elected officials are out of touch, government is too big, spending is out of control, the Obamacare program has itself been a train wreck from its inception. Obamacare seems destined to create fewer patients through neglect rather than providing more cures. The VA system looks like a good way to rid the government of too many patients.

Worse than anything else imaginable, heroes from Vietnam, Korea, Mideast Wars, and elsewhere, after killing the enemy and surviving—are being killed one at a time by the VA System. Some would say these war survivors are dying in a VA system supposedly designed to keep them alive. Nobody, after spending $160 billion per year supposedly on Veterans, can tell us why they are neglected. Any Joe on the street could figure out how to save veterans for $160 billion a year!

The people of America who choose to pay attention see the federal government as incompetent because they are paying attention and they know more than most. We have no voice. We find our government exchanging five of the nastiest Taliban Officers at the top of their game, from Gitmo for one deserter PFC, while a patriotic and heroic former Marine rots in a Mexican jail. . Additionally, and this is the worst: *"too many of US are too lazy to hold government accountable, and too many of our finest are on the take."*

The government has created a train wreck. Additionally, corporate leaches have infiltrated our government, and they demand their take of the proceeds. We have record unemployment; illegal aliens are smiling as they take American jobs; cunning kids are enrolling for US benefits at the border; an unsustainable status quo supports special interests over the people's interests—and when we look to the future we see a public education system that intentionally creates dummmies with a *common core* that is rotten to the core, and intentionally so.

Today's high school graduates are so dummm that they don't seem to mind being called dummmies. They expect whatever job they get to consist of drill and practice tests just like the *common core*, so they can do well.

What if jobs are essay questions requiring thought instead of rote memorization of answers to unasked questions? What if they are not multiple choice or T/F deals? Can the test oriented student of today succeed with just the Common Core? Scrooge would sum it up with a hearty "Bah Humbug." It is that bad and perhaps even worse!

We have the poorest economy since the depression; excessive welfare and income redistribution; institutionalized lying; a corrupt state-loving press that carries water for government; a debt large enough to kill America; huge student debt stopping graduates' success; tyranny v. democracy; government lawlessness; freedom and liberty in jeopardy; American stagnation, and a big loss of America's world prestige. But, who is keeping track. Unfortunately, the free press, which is supposed to keep things from going south, has gone south.

And, on top of that, we have a top leader who learns about what's happening in his administration from the daily paper. Yet this same supposedly competent person does not chastise or fire his advisors whose missions are to keep him apprised. Everybody gets a free ride with no accountability. It is that bad. One could not be creating as much harm to America if they actually intended to do so.

Maybe I am wrong. Today's news brought forth a different President Obama, one who is smarter than the guy who finds out about America from reading the daily news. It seems the President got sick of that finger being put in his eye.

Just when you think you can actually imprint the President's action permanently in a book, he pivots, and past truths are no longer true. Maybe they never were true? Who knows? I bet only the President's advisors know for sure. This President seems to be either lying all the time or most of the time, and sometimes feels compelled to alter the truth.

After being the paper reader who gets the news days after all other Americans get it, Mr. Obama told supporters [at a Democratic fundraiser] that he doesn't watch the news because, "Whatever they're reporting about, usually I know." That contrasts with the explanations that the President and his aides have given from scandals in the past few years ranging from long wait times and deaths at the VA, to the IRS targeting tea party groups, to the Fast and Furious gun-running operation, and the Department of Justice spying on news reporters.

I suspect a former George Bush staffer, probably an illegal alien, is hiding in the shadows of the administration, and at selected times offers multiple versions of various crises without any of the Obama team knowing such insidious news activities are taking place.
For the second time in the Obama administration, and the third time since the Jimmy Carter days, the corrupt press is creating stories to explain why their president is not effective. In the waning months of 2014, like two such efforts in the past they are promulgating a story that no regular human being can handle all of the duties of the presidency, period. Admittedly, this current President has messianic qualities but perhaps, according to those pushing this line of reasoning,

even that is not enough to handle such a complicated office. Because Bill Clinton was merely a Lothario, and not a really bad president, this promulgated story, about the impossibility of being a good president, was never released during the Clinton years.

It is not the presidency per se; but it is big government that has become such a problem that it can never again be the solution. The presidency, with competent staffing, and a strong and representative Congress can definitely meet the challenges of being modern government leaders.

Our long term hope for replacement players in government and in industry, our youth, do need some help to get back in the game. They go through colleges in huge numbers only to be unemployed and sacked with debt. The hole is so big, few can ever become whatever they might have been able to become in years past.

Today's emerging adults have no clue what life is about and they are incented by their mentors unfortunately, to actually protest for ideological reasons that they, themselves may not even hold.

For example, they have been convinced by their elders at the universities to condemn American heroes such as Condoleezza Rice and Dr. Ben Carson when they come visit their institutions, for purposes of congratulations to the student body.

Rutgers University, for example in 2013 picked a boardwalk babe, Snooki, rather than an American who loves America to give them their final addresses at their Universities. Rutgers faculty and students applauded this mind-numbing choice.

One year later they put up such a stink about an American hero being named their speaker that Condoleezza Rice was forced to cancel because of the nastiness against her. The University stood by as its esteemed communist faculty deluded students into thinking Karl Marx would have been a better choice.

Students in most universities, and I might suggest, all big universities, are guided by communist faculty members, who know it all, especially when dressed in their finest plumage at commencement ceremonies. With guidance from those who hate America, students begin to think they know it all, and that America really sucks! Meanwhile honest parents admit that they have no clue what happens to their children once they reach the campus.

Young millennials somehow are taught in universities to love leftism and progressivism and big government. Yet, when they graduate, 85% find themselves going back home to live with conservative moms and dads because the progressive left big government economy offers them no job opportunities at all. Mom and dad of course did not save for junior's return, and the allowance demands are even greater than when in college.

Eventually students at home who are now ahem, *graduates* either become wards of the state or they break towards conservatism and assure their own rights as in the Bill of Rights.

You may recall at graduation time in 2014, the administrators and the communist faculty and student lemmings at the State University of New Jersey, Rutgers, embarrassed Dr. Condoleezza Rice, a major US historical figure. They were nasty and unwelcoming and protested her choice as commencement speaker. Rice appropriately rescinded her acceptance.

Their idea of free speech is that it is OK only if it is approved thought. More and more universities are carving out very small areas of their campus in which free speech may be practiced. In the past all of America, including all college campuses, every inch, were free speech zones.

The student loan burden prevents former student borrowers, trained by communist elite, from buying homes, cars, and having a family. The communist teachers think none of this is necessary anyway unless provided by the state.

We live in an age in which only retirees in their 90's can afford honeymoon cottages while looking for their next spouse. As many as 37 million student loan borrowers are too broke to engage in basic life. College loans, instead of lifting people to the top, have created a new race to the bottom,

On the International stage, America has become a bad actor. Allies can no longer take US on our word. Israel, the continual voice of reason in the Mideast is being bullied by Vietnam Veteran John Kerry, current US Secretary of State, to capitulate to the many rockets from Hamas sent into their suburbs to kill innocent people. Kerry wants to claim a diplomatic victory but cares nothing about assuring the right team wins the engagement. . Why not let Israel win a victory and end the conflict once and for all. Why is the US preventing Israel from protecting themselves for the long haul. Has the president read the papers yet about this tragedy?

To make it worse, frustrated zealots from the Left are making sure nobody gives America a break on the world stage. The Leader of the Free world is hell bent on making the rest of the world strong by making America weak. He highlights perceived American weakness and when he apologizes for America, it does little to command respect for our country.

Nobody in the world gives America standing ovations anymore. Nobody asks us for curtain calls. Our leaders turn their backs on our friends and seem to pay homage to our enemies. How is this?

In mid 2014, we gave five top command level terrorists in exchange for a POW who was a PFC when captured and promoted twice in captivity, eventually to Sergeant. The POW is accused of desertion, and the Congress accused the President of not following the law in the exchange. Does anybody want to make America right again?

The President is now threatening to go the Executive order route with student loans. Though something should be done, it is not right for the President to go it alone. The Constitution and the Bill of Rights are not in one man's control.

Smaller and weaker countries such as Russia, Iran, and North Korea continue to push US around and laugh at US, and our only response is to see if somehow we may have offended them. How many take-downs of Malaysian planes will it take for our enemies to begin taking US passenger planes out of the sky?

The new America, rather than rattling our enemies by promising and delivering quick doom for bad behavior, shows its greatness by counting the number of hits on a *hashtag of **bring our girls home,*** when no Americans are missing.

Our misinformed experts expect terrorists to cower when the number of twitter resends hits a million. We also refuse to discuss why four Americans, including the Ambassador, were permitted to die in Benghazi when the military says they were prepared to save them. We accept too many lies from our government. Perhaps none of us understand the rights the Founders gave us?

We have an administration that blames the Christian Government of Nigeria for not reaching out enough to the Muslim killers who kidnapped 300 girls as sex slaves. Boko Haram had captured and killed 49 boys just a few weeks before. The captors boldly announced they would sell the girls on the sex slave market, and the US is powerless in its feeble response. Unless you are a communist progressive liberal and then, you see real power in the hashtag!

Hundreds of thousands of illegal aliens have been invited to our country by President Obama in mid-2014 and long before in what some now call a humanitarian crisis. Others say it is the Left's idea of removing the borders completely to encourage more poor and needy to come to America to increase the votes for big government and progressive policies.

Conservative military leaders suggest that it is dangerous for America as many terrorists are entering through the open borders while border guards are changing diapers.

I find myself asking the same questions as most sane Americans. What has happened to our good sense? Should there not be a set of laws written by sane people and enforced by people who have taken oaths to do so. Such insane acts should not be permitted to occur without retribution?

Why do our representatives and today's President not represent America? Why does nobody pay attention to the Bill of Rights? Do we know our rights? Can knowledge of our rights help us in this upside down world? I would not have written this book if I thought it could not.

For me, these are the worst days of America that I have ever witnessed. Yet, the leadership and our government seem to have no problems that need solutions. Clear-thinking Americans look at today's leaders as buffoons, without the wherewithal to tie their own shoes. These leaders would like all Americans to be happy in a state of mediocrity, rather than having an opportunity to become outstanding. "Don't worry: Be Happy!"

If you have been paying attention, and I sure hope you have been as it is a civic duty, you know that there are even more issues than the exhaustive list we just walked you through. Isn't that a shame on US? I think this is the reason that you bought this book. Thank you very much.

The Constitution is a survivor's guide to dealing with corrupt politicians. The *Bill of Rights* is an extra edition to assure that the people come first, and the government last.

We are on the right side and thankfully we are on the same side, and together we can all help arrest control of our leftist progressive government back from perpetrators wishing to destroy US.

We first must understand what is going on and we then must understand our rights. Even before you and I and everybody else are on board, just like Howard Beale, we must start the first wave of solutions by opening our windows all the way and shouting as loud as we all can: "I am mad as hell, and I am not going to take this anymore."

Then, make sure that you talk to all of the other "dummmies" out there that you know—people like you and I and others, and let's help them know that unless we all fully engage in America, when we wake up from our deep fog, there may be no America left for our progeny.

We will have blown it for sure if that is permitted to happen.

Chapter 3   The USA is a Constitutional Republic!

A Representative Democracy

The Constitution prescribes that the US is a representative democracy, which as you probably already know means that along with having an elected chief executive (president) and a constitution, also makes the US a *Republic*. The pledge of allegiance, which was once mandatory reading in US schools when there was no question that even the government believed that Americans should love America, notes the words: "…and to the *Republic* for which it stands." Our great, and wonderful and rightfully proud country is both a representative democracy and a republic.

When we think of the very important notion that "America is a representative democracy," watching the "clowns" from both parties, who occupy our central government, it is a sane question to ask if this is really true.

The song, "Is that all there is?" comes to mind. We are nothing like our parents and nothing like our Founders. We have reason to be ashamed of our government, but then again, our country today is so far off the Founders' mark that even shame is not politically correct.

A representative democracy is the foundation of America. However, what makes America—America is that we are also a Republic—the finest form of government ever brought forth from mankind. The Bill of Rights, the subject of this book is just an add-on to an unending list of inalienable rights for the people—you and I, and none for government.

Don't be duped that government is the answer. Government is the people's slave and when it goes awry as today, it must be reined in. But, you already know that as you are one of the chosen to read this book about your rights as a citizen of the USA.

We also have a set of laws, beginning with our Constitution, the primary law of the land. These laws govern all people and all politicians in perpetuity—as long as *we* choose to hold them accountable.

The simple definition of a republic (from Latin -- res publica), is as follows: a state in which supreme power is held by the people and their elected representatives, and which has an elected or nominated president rather than a monarch.

In practice in a republic, the government is ruled by elected leaders run according to law. The law in our country is **The Constitution**. Unlike a democracy, a republic is not based on majority rule. The law of the land, a Constitution gives the minority a voice. Moreover, the majority cannot decide in such a government that Brian W. Kelly, your humble author, can be summarily killed since he does not measure up. In a republic, it takes lots more than that and that is why real laws are important to us all.

Our biggest and most important laws within the US Constitution are written so that the government cannot hurt US or impose its will upon US without our explicit consent. Our country was founded by very some smart people and they knew that without constraints on any government, which could potentially go wild, the people would not win.

The constraints in the Constitution are implicit in that all of the rights are owned by the people, and only those rights explicitly given to government are for the government. The only purpose of the Bill of Rights is so that Americans know where their starter set of rights begin. Government has no additional rights.

Let me repeat. Government has no rights other than those granted by law to the government by the people. The people have all the rights. A government that subjugates the people for its purposes is expressly forbidden in these United States of America.

This great body of law known as the Constitution therefore makes politicians and others in government fear a backlash when they attempt to deny the people, even just one person our liberty and freedom. In a pure democracy, if the majority decided that you or I should be killed, nothing would necessarily stop it if it were to be. But, in a republic such as ours, it is the rule of law which prevails and the rule of law starts with the Constitution.

It seems for sure that many in our nation today, mostly on the far left, are trying real hard to kill America's America by demeaning the Constitution and the Bill of Rights in particular. With majority rule in a pure democracy, the only problem is that you may not be of the majority. Then what?

You more than likely selected this book to help fight them off. If the Courts stay honest, and that is not assured, the people will always prevail because the laws are on our side.

If you could figure any way to put an unmovable grip on corrupt politicians, right now or in the future, would you not do so? The founders of America put such a stranglehold on all political agents of the future when they wrote and adopted the US Constitution, the greatest body of law ever written in any civilization. Government has no inalienable rights. Such rights are reserved for the people, and many of those are listed in the Bill of Rights!

Of course, if we the people do not know what is written in the Constitution, it cannot help us much. Can it? So, it is time for all Americans who have not been paying attention to stop being dummmies, and political sport for the elite. It is time to rule America as our birthright as citizens of this great country commands US to do. Let somebody else eat cake!

And, so, my fellow Americans, that is the number one reason that in order to form a more perfect union of the original thirteen colonies / states, and with more states expected after the first thirteen, our Forefathers built the finest Constitution ever fashioned by the pen of human beings.

The Bible, from the hand of God, may be the greatest story ever told in the greatest book ever written, but the Constitution is as good as it gets for the goodness of man, written by the hands of our first patriots. Surely, this document was written with the guidance of God.

In this day and age, there are everyday attempts by the government which is controlled by the far left, to undermine our lasting Republic, which is an almost pure constitutional representative democracy. As noted, the attacks most often come from the left side of the political spectrum.

Democracy is the opposite of communism

The ideology of the progressive left favors Marxism and its simpler forms of socialism and communism. Since Americans do not vote for socialists, communists, or Marxists, these are things that nobody other than a crooked politician should want. But, even though they desire these ends, they will not openly speak about the communistic state which they espouse.

If you are unaware of this in today's government, it is time you considered paying more attention. No politician wanting to be elected will admit that they are more communist than American. Yet, as much as it pains me to tell you, unfortunately, they are!

These overtures, which demean the Constitution, the fabric of our democracy, originate from corrupt politicians who have been caught up in the leftist movement, which would like to end capitalism, and bring on a socialist / communist order in which they were the leaders. They want to replace the American Dream, and all the dreams of *We the People*!

Our Republic as noted is a representative democracy constrained by laws with the Constitution being the biggest constraint—and that is good. Yet, we do have representatives. Most represent themselves, and a good portion of them would like the Constitution to be abolished so they can lord over us, without constraints.

One midnight, I asked myself one of those haunting questions: "Isn't it about time that we real Americans actually had some real "representation" from the so-called representatives in our so-called representative government? I said to myself: "Yes it is!" It doesn't have to be a dream. If we believe, it can easily again be made a reality. And, we should scream it out at the polling places and at our representative's offices as often as we can. We should accept nothing less. If we choose not to do so, they win. That means we lose.

The people have the responsibility of keeping government honest!

It is up to all people in this great country to understand our laws, first the Constitution, of which the Bill of Rights is key, and then to pay attention that our leaders follow those laws. When they do not follow the laws of the land, we must learn to send them home every two, four, or six years, as determined by the term lengths as set forth in Constitution for our House (2 years), the President (4 years), and the Senate (6 years) respectively. They deserve no second chances.

To say it more clearly: We get to throw the bums out and replace them with people of character on a regular basis; so don't give up! That is why our government has worked well for over 225 years. When we get bad apples, we throw them away by voting them out. Of course that means we must vote in order for our choices to matter. And we must be willing to vote our own local representatives in the House or the Senate out of office when they choose to not do their jobs by sticking up for America. .

Representatives are of the people?

Though the representatives are supposed to come from the people, a type of political class of elites has come about and seldom do we get to vote for representatives anymore, who are truly of the people. By understanding America better, and especially by understanding our Constitution and its built-in Bill of Rights, Americans have a far better chance of bringing good and honest government back to the people.

The way it now works, there is far too much separation between US, the electors, and them, the elected officials. Most officials choose to live in gated communities, unaware of what is happening on our streets. How many of our fine elected have invited the poor Children from Central America from the immigration crisis of 2014 into their homes? Yet, they ask us to bring them into our neighborhoods and pay for their every need. How's that?

The Constitution provides that elected officials are given the task to coordinate our pooled resources for the intended benefit of "everyone." Everyone is this country until recently meant all US citizens. But everyone is often not included? We see politicians taking credit for spending treasury dollars on things that simply buy themselves votes. Nobody wants this and so it is up to all of US—We the People—to change it.

Do our representatives in the second decade of the twenty-first century have a genuinely compelling concern for the people and our government or is this simply a stilted notion of Nirvana?

Most of US do not know that Nirvana is the name in Buddhism as its final goal— a transcendent state in which there is neither suffering, desire, nor sense of self; and the subject is released from the effects of karma and the cycle of death and rebirth.

If it is not Nirvana, perhaps what we are experiencing is a Disney-like Utopian myth perpetrated on US by these same "benevolent yet corrupt politicians?" Of course, it may be that our representatives do not care because we do not hold them accountable. We elect them even when they are knaves—even thieves and criminals. Do any of US think US politicians really care about the people they have sworn to represent?

I propose the latter. Our government is wholly unaccountable to *We the People*. Today, our government rejects the fundamental principles of our Founding and has no real legitimacy the further it drifts from the precepts of the Constitution.

The US was not designed this way. The Constitution is the blueprint for our Country's design. It was designed by a group of artisans to not only represent their artistic touch, but to be held as the behavioral creed of the people, for the people, and by the people, forever. What thinking human being blessed to be part of America, could ask for anything more?

If you think that life, freedom, liberty, and the ability to pursue your own happiness are simple notions, and *givens* in any civilization, get out your thinking cap, and think again. Why do people from all over the world crash our gates just to

get in? Americans are exceptional in that we have full
freedom and liberty in our country, and with that we can
exceed all limits of ordinary expectation. Go to any other
country, and this exception no longer applies.

Traditionally, the USA has been the freest nation in the
world with rights withheld from government and rights given
to the people by our Constitution. Today as our country's
foundation is being threatened from within, more than likely
you are reading about the Bill of Rights and the Constitution
so you can help protect your rights as well as this great
nation, which provides them.

If you had to give something up—which would you first give
up? Your freedom? Your life? Your liberty? Your family? Or
your ability to do what you need to do to be happy? The
sanest answer of course is "none of the above."

Who could ask for anything more than being an American?
Ask the last arriving immigrant why they come here! We are
free! But, if Americans do not care about our founding
precepts, maybe our freedom, our lives, our liberty, our
families, and our ability to do what we need to be happy, will
be taken from us one day—perhaps in the not-too-distant
future.

If the design of our nation, America, which the founders
labored to create is so great, you might ask, why is it that our
current lawmakers ignore it? They have no trouble going with
the flow and committing US to years of debt without even
taking the time to read the debt-ridden legislation for which
they vote. Neither the Constitution nor the Founders would
approve of what our representatives, including our President,
have done to our country.

Even worse, members of Congress, our alleged civil servants,
the supposed representatives of the people, are able to get
away without doing their jobs, while collecting more and

more remuneration for their main act of hurting the American people at large.

The true answer to that question [Why is it that our current lawmakers ignore the laws of the nation?] is very unfortunate for Americans. There is tacit collaboration in undermining the principles of our Democratic Republic by our supposed representatives, their supporters, the special interests, and their corporate interests.

We the people now come last. They think we are not paying attention. Maybe we have not been paying enough attention but don't you agree that—that is about to end. *Pay attention* is about to become the motto of the free in America! Let the subjugated wish for more government! Let the free actively seek to keep our freedom and liberty!

Chapter 4   Early America Populated by Immigrants

Legitimate immigration was necessary

Americans are all pro-immigration to the extent of our laws. If Americans were not pro-immigration for example, Columbus and his shipmates and their families more than likely would have withered away from disease or cold winters or they would have lost their battles with the Indians. Additionally, all fifty states; at least the mainland's forty-eight, would probably now have Indian names, such as Redskins, and they would be run by the same financial wizards who run today's highly successful casinos.

After the USA was in operation as a country with a Constitution for just several years, its population was not much more than 4 million people. This is just a million more people than the annual flow of illegal immigrants from south of the border. This was of course before the illegal children revolution brought to us in our time by our current President and his DREAM executive orders, because Congress did not give him his way.

On March 26, 1790, almost 225 years ago, the second session of the first Congress (operating under the Constitution with a real House and a real Senate) approved the new nation's initial effort to create the rules under which foreign-born persons could become U.S. citizens.

After these laws, from this point on, our borders were not open per se, and we had these laws (rules) for how those wishing to be Americans could come to visit or to become Americans. All Americans after this point who immigrated were to follow the law of the land. The law did not suggest that they violate the law, step on US soil, and then hide because nobody would bug them.

The Naturalization Act of 1790 specified that "any alien, being a free white person," could apply for citizenship, so long as he or she lived in the United States for at least two years, and in the state where the application was filed for at least a year. The new law also provided that "children of citizens of the United States that may be born ... out of the limits of the United States shall be considered as natural born citizens."

In effect, it left out indentured servants, slaves, and most women. It also mandated that one must "absolutely and entirely renounce and abjure all allegiance and fidelity to every foreign Prince, Potentate, State or Sovereignty." Though these terms were seen as quite generous, still the law denied the right to naturalize to "persons whose fathers have never been resident in the United States." This was a law of the US!

Immigration law was becoming more important and the laws have been changed several times since 1790. For example, in 1795, as anti-immigrant feeling began to grow, the necessary period of residence to become a citizen was increased from two to five years. Immigration law became more firm as the nation aged. Americans wanted America to be America, not a suburb of a country that wanted to be independent of America's laws.

Enter special interests, who like to bypass laws and have their friendly "owned" politicians let them get away with it.

Regarding immigration, you already know that there are two major special interests. The first special interest is the Democratic Party, which believes that if all illegal foreign nationals were to be immediately made citizens, the

Democrat Party would never lose another election. That is a great motivator to bring all foreigners in immediately and make them all citizens of this nation.

And, so, even though they have taken American jobs and driven down the average weekly wage, your Democratic Representatives in Congress still advocate amnesty and citizenship for them, promising less prosperity for all American citizens. And, unfortunately, most Americans, not seeing that the representatives have become communists, looking for a poor and continually underserved underclass, they will vote them back into office at their own peril.

Their major concern as corrupt politicians see it is that the Democrat members of Congress get reelected and another Democrat president is elected next time and every time. That really is the only concern of the ruling party. Bringing in poor people from south of the border, who feed from our welfare system, taking tax dollars from those with minimal incomes, assures the Democratic politicians of the illegal's votes, and it is paid for by the working slobs who happen to pay taxes.

The second special interest is also against the people. They do not gain at the ballot box. However, illegal foreign nationals do provide huge gains in the wallets of American Business. American businesses love paying the smallest wage possible and since illegal foreign nationals work for peanuts, there is a perfect marriage of needs.

Traditional Republicans have great alliances with businesses. The only groups, who align with the majority of Americans and who oppose blanket amnesty and who are 100% pro-American citizen philosophically, are conservatives, such as those in the TEA Party.

If you get a wrenching feeling in your stomach when you read TEA Party, it is because the corrupt US media has sensitized you into their bias. They do not tell you they are communists and they do not give a damn whether you or your children do well in America simply because they know you won't like them anymore.

So, the media lies about the TEA Party and anything that hurts their progressive / socialist agenda. They do not deliver the real news to Americans yet most of US forgive them for their lack of honesty anyway. Since they all have big popular names, they think the small people like US will take their slop and believe it. And, enough did in 2012 to re-elect the first incompetent president.

If you are a hard and fast left-winger, the actions of the press may please you but if you simply love America, this should enrage you. We all need to know our rights to fight a dishonest press, knowing that most of our rights stem from the Bill of Rights ad the others directly from the Constitution.

Conservatives differ on immigration with elitist Republicans, and opportunist Democrats. No American citizen suffering from the worst economy since the depression would be asking the government to invite in more wage lowering workers. How does adding to the worker pool help American citizens get jobs?

Thomas J. Donahue, President of the US Chamber of Congress (C of C) recently told Republican lawmakers that "if they do not pass amnesty, the Republicans shouldn't bother to run a candidate in 2016." The C of C cares nothing about workers' salaries but cares a lot about corporate profits. Donohue expects lawmakers to pass amnesty rather than forego campaign funding from the Chamber.

The US Senate, long controlled by Democrats, passed a global amnesty bill in early 2014. The goal was to nail Americans by giving their jobs to foreigners. Democrats do not like American citizens in need, who do not want to accept government help. The Democrats, of which I admit I am one, have been pressuring the House of Representatives to do the same throughout 2014.

So far, the conservatives in the House have blocked a vote, though Speaker Boehner a, who must live in an all-white neighborhood, appears always ready to cave to the more powerful Obama and the Republican elite. This vote may happen any day before the 2014 elections and if it does, I for one am voting straight Democrat.

At least the Democrats are honest about killing America. If the Republican house passes the terrible Senate Amnesty Bill, and it becomes law, the people have no choice but to throw out both houses of Congress and start over. The people have lots of power when we "pay attention."

The immigration issue is being put forth early in this book to demonstrate that our legislators care more about other factors such as reelection and donations than they do about the people. President Obama, who theoretically cannot run again, has been on 400 fund raisers so far since being elected. President Bush for example went to about 200 at this time in his presidency. Nobody elected a campaigner in chief but that is what we got.

We have more than enough illegal immigrants and citizens out of work in the country right now or else our real unemployment picture would not look so bad. Why bring more "*slave labor*" into the country when we know it will make the problem of making ends meet for American families even worse?

Perhaps too many of US, until things got this bad, had been hoping George would do it! Well, George Washington, one of our finest patriots is long gone, and unless you know of a recent George with the time, it is up to US to do it. Washington and Bush are gone. Those in Congress who bow to special interests should be made to take their final bows.

And, by the way, the two George Bush's did not get it done either. But, today's President and his Attorney General don't even try. They are on the other team v. Americans. They choose not to enforce any immigration laws.

They do not follow the law of the land, the Constitution. They pay lip service to the Bill of Rights except for the Second Amendment which they think should not exist. This is tyranny, yet with a divided Congress, it is tough to get action on behalf of the people.

This book is not about immigration, but it is about the Constitution and more specifically, the Bill of Rights. Both of these documents help all Americans to know that the laws are made for Americans to benefit. To demonstrate the lawlessness of the current administration and the disdain they have even for war heroes, here are a few anecdotes.

Without a scintilla of Constitutional authority, just recently, today's President ordered well over 30,000 imprisoned criminals in illegal status to simply be released so "they could be reunited with their families in the US." Among them are rapists and murderers. The homicide and rape victims got no say. The criminals were released from prison into the US— not deported.

They are back on the streets of the US. Did we really need 30,000 more criminals on our streets? Today's President thinks we should cajole and love the more than 50,000,000 souls in our illegal population, and he acts like our laws do not apply to him or to foreigners. Meanwhile 30,000 American citizens in prison were not released to be with their families. I agree American criminals should not be released but neither should foreign national criminals.

There is another true story that shows how ridiculous it is for the US to bend over backwards to coddle 30,000 criminals with illegal foreign national status. Mexican authorities punish Americans in Mexico for the smallest of infractions and will not free them even when there is national outrage in the USA.

Right now, as I am writing this book, for example, Mexican authorities are holding Sergeant Andrew Tahmooressi, a Marine war hero from Florida. He stood trial but to no avail so far. A Mexican judge in July 2014 sent him back to prison awaiting another appearance in August.

US outrage was expressed in a headline from Memorial Day Weekend, 2014: "Leave no man behind: Why is Team Obama unable to bring home Marine held in Mexico?" How inept a leader is a president who would like us to think he owns Mexico, yet he will not lift a finger to help a US Marine or go to the US border to see *the immigration crisis of children* first hand. . Later many were wondering how today's President could free a deserter from the Taliban and completely ignore the plight of this hero Marine.

While on the battlefield, this brave Marine saved eight fellow Marines from the Taliban, and in a separate incident he saved a Marine from bleeding to death after he stepped on an IED and lost his legs. Tahmooressi also suffered a concussion when his vehicle hit an IED.

On March 20, 2014, the U.S. Department of Veterans Affairs diagnosed this young soldier with Post-Traumatic Stress Disorder (PTSD). Yet, even our President cannot get him freed from a Mexican Jail. Maybe the President has not yet made the call, or maybe he simply does not like Marines? Or maybe he has no power? Who really knows?

This unlucky former Marine simply mis-navigated the San Diego highways and ended up in Mexico. Rather than being treated with respect and returned, this hero Marine was apprehended and incarcerated and more than three months, he is still there fearing for his life in a dreadful and very dangerous Mexican prison.

After a night in which he avoided death from a prison "Hit Squad," he was placed in solitary confinement with his four limbs chained to a bed. We treat no illegal foreign nationals with such cruelty. Maybe Mexico is trying to teach the US how to treat border violators?

Some of our rights spawned by the Constitution come about because the legislative branch (Congress,) formed by the Constitution creates additional laws. For example, no American can be captured and held by a foreign government unjustly. Here is how this law reads.

U.S. Code, Title 22, Chapter 23, Section 1732. It is entitled, "Release of citizens imprisoned by foreign governments."

Whenever it is made known to the President that any citizen of the United States has been unjustly deprived of his liberty by or under the authority of any foreign government, it shall be the duty of the President forthwith to demand of that government the reasons of such imprisonment; and if it appears to be wrongful and in violation of the rights of American citizenship, the President shall forthwith demand the release of such citizen, and if the release so demanded is unreasonably delayed or refused, the President shall use such means, not amounting to acts of war and not otherwise prohibited by law, as he may think necessary and proper to obtain or effectuate the release; and all the facts and proceedings relative thereto shall as soon as practicable be communicated by the President to Congress.

There is no excuse that Americans should accept for the president to not have gotten this Marine released. Perhaps the President, who sometimes learns about what's happening in the country by reading the daily newspaper, rather than being the Chief Executive and Commander in Chief, will use his old Sergeant Schultz standby excuse. Perhaps he has not been reading the papers and thus he has an out in not upholding another of our laws simply by saying as he does all too often. "I know nothing. Nobody told me." What a shame! Congress must force the President's hand to do his job.

Can it be that too many of US and too many of our friends have been Bill of Rights and other privileges "dummies" for too long? Perhaps understanding our rights and government limitations from the Bill of Rights and the Constitution, as well as your exhortations to all your friends will help many Americans awaken to what happens in a country in which government, rather than the people, has the stronger hand. Remember when government officials do not follow the people's commands, we get to un-elect them or impeach them. I'd say it is our play now!

Chapter 5   Does The Bill of Rights Matter?

Americans are too trustworthy?

Our representatives are in office far too long and they gain relationships with other politicians who make up the ruling class. Instead of thinking about the folks in Danbury or Wilkes-Barre, or Clarks-Summit, or Santa Rosa, or Chicago, or Avoca, or Great Plains, or Orlando, our esteemed politicians begin to think they belong in Washington DC, not their home territories.

The social life in DC is lots better than most home towns, and our devoted representatives get to rub elbows with the hoity-toity, and the progressive Marxist communists that do not exist in their home areas. They get corrupted. All of a sudden they are important, and being from Podunk or Plymouth does not matter. They begin to like the trappings of Washington more than being with their loved ones back in their home states.

And they try to please the lobbyists and the communists and others on the other team. They want to be liked and they want something in return that they don't get from the home town folks. Sometimes it is gifts; sometimes it is invitations to the best parties; and sometimes it is the promise of a great job if not reelected. The longer they are in Congress or in politics per se, the greater the opportunity for corruption.

Unfortunately for all Americans, the new "important" relationships trump the notion of fair representation for the people (US) from back home. When they take their oaths of office and they promise to represent US, most are sincere at the time. That may be the last time.

Once they come to Washington, they experience the trappings and the temptations. And, because humans are only human, way too many of our finest stray from the mark and contribute to the re-creation of a country of which few thinking Americans are proud today.

Yet, we Americans are either too kind or not enough self-assured that we trust them even after innumerable lies and self-aggrandizements. We can't believe they would do "that," yet they do. So, like dummmies, we go ahead and we call them hizzoner or herronner and we reelect them because we think they really cannot be as bad as they are.

Ladies and gentlemen, they are that bad. Stop electing them. Their biggest fear is that someday all Americans will understand the Constitution chapter and verse. On that day, we have all the rights, and they have zero.

Think about our Forefathers, especially George Washington, who guided our troops in the revolution against England's tyranny. Think about honest Abe Lincoln, who freed the slaves and saved the union. They would weep to see what their political successors, our representatives, have done to our nation.

So, our fair haired representatives (figure of speech) choose to represent themselves and their special interests, rather than the areas of the country that sent them to the Congress of the USA to represent the people. Perhaps a dose of Lincoln's "honesty," is all that is needed to save the day. Wouldn't that be nice?

Our "honorable," do not even seem to care for our well-being. They care for their leadership positions, which make them big shots, and they care for themselves for sure.

Unfortunately, they just can't get it into their heads that we the people are the reason they are in their positions in the first place.

We the people are the employers of all members of Congress, and they serve at our pleasure. The more we all understand that the tighter the reins we can place on errant politicians, the more the people are in charge. It is not too late. The Constitution is our guide and it is our license to rid ourselves of a poor government.

We must understand the Constitution and the Bill of Rights in order for them to work again for US and for America. The last thing we should consider doing is to permit the corrupt politicians that we unfortunately have already elected to serve the people, to disembody our Constitution through legislation or through executive actions.

Then again, maybe a lot of the problem is our fault since we do not check them out well enough before we slam them into office. To make it simple to understand this notion—if there is a rotten piece of fish in the market and we select it for dinner, whose fault is it when it doesn't taste so good and our guests get sick? So, when we pick a rotten person to represent US—whose fault is that? You see, we do not have to be dummmies. We simply choose to be.

Does it matter whether the government is controlled by Democrats or Republicans? Democratic leaders have become socialist progressives, just this side of communists over the past several years. The Democrats at home are not far leftists but their leaders are. Republicans still seem to love the American way and are not moving the country towards communism. Our country's demise rate grows at a faster clip when leftist progressive communists are in office. When Republicans take over, though it lessens, it does go to zero as it should because a number of Republicans have become progressive also. That is not good!

So, right now at least, Republicans, especially conservative Republicans are a better choice for America than Democrats. As a conservative Democrat myself, that is very tough for me to say. I wish it were not so. The best thing for America is to vote for conservatives, even if they are Democrat. But, the facts show most conservatives are either Republican or Libertarian.

The people are always short changed on the notion of representation and honesty. Honesty is the first thing to go when a representative must lie in order to get the extra benefits their positions can deliver.

When has any incumbent representative run effectively on honesty? Is that because we the people do not care about honesty or are we all smart enough to know that they are kidding. We do not need the Constitution to know that but it might help us to be more honest if we knew and loved the Constitution just a little bit more. Either way it is our fault. We voted most of these 545 miscreants to run our government. We get the government we deserve.

Somebody once said that if you like your honesty, you will be able to keep it and it should save you about $2500.00 per year. But I jest, yet my jest is serious. Do you know who that guy was? Now, helping fight a guy like that is a great place in which we can use our knowledge of the Bill of Rights and the even greater rights provided by the US Constitution.

OK, nobody said that exactly but some president at some time in the last four years told Americans that they could keep their doctors, their health policies, and they could save $2500.00. I am not kidding. He is still telling lies because no person in Congress feels strong enough to buck the low information gullible American people and take him on. They think they can get elected again if they retreat from their sworn duty. It is up to us to prove them wrong by throwing the bums out. It really is that simple.

My objective in this book as in many others, which I write, is not to have you know who said that or to get you upset whether he or she did or did not say it. I just want you to think about what the Founders promised and what good the American government had been delivering to the people before the liars took charge.

There is a chasm. We the people can fix that. Learning the precepts of the Bill of Rights, expanded further by the inherent rights in the Constitution and the Declaration of Independence, can inspire US to get that task done.

My objective with this book is to help smarten you up so that guys like that, whether they are the president or not, do not get to treat you like a chump. Each time I write about this topic, I get smarter also as we all must keep learning all our lives and we must be watchful of tyranny so that we can keep our freedom and our liberties.

America is built on fairness, goodness, and individual strength. We are not supposed to give politicians an even break. The Constitution is our law and it is our obligation to pay attention so our rights are not violated by grabby self-centered politicians. If you happen to be in this low information / overly nice category, thank you for visiting this book. I hope that through these writings, you will become a better American.

The low information gullible people in America must smarten up or we are all toast. Everybody's vote counts the same. When those who choose to not pay attention vote, it is a big plus for dirty politicians and a big loss for real Americans.

When you have the time, please finish reading this book, and you will understand how smart you can be and how much power you can wield against those who care nothing about you or me, or America. Always keep your eye on the ball and do not give the ball up to an opponent just because they lie and they schmooze you.

The Bill of Rights 4 Dummmies, is written so that we can all know the truth even when the corrupt media lies to our faces as they do every day. The not-so-free, very dishonest and corrupt statist press provides propaganda for the government and too many gullible Americans sop it up as if it is the truth. The media would have us all believe in the "*Tooth Fairy.*" Any of US that live by believing their lies, are simply un-smartened chumps.

Regardless of which party is responsible for the mess, Americans are on edge anticipating that somehow, because there are big problems, we will all get nailed by one or another of them in one way or another. Many of US think that we will lose our jobs, lose our ability to work full time, lose our health insurance policies, and not be able to afford the new government issued policies coming our way.

Unfortunately, too many of us look to government, the creators of all American problems, as the only place where there is a possible solution. Not true! Never go to a problem creator for a solution!

When I was growing up, it was not this way. It is time we went back to the better days when there was a real American Dream for everybody.

We may get sick and we may die because of the "Affordable Care Act." Thank God the President is not under Obamacare so at least he will be available for a eulogy at any of our funerals.

Illegal immigration and amnesty is another of the bad jokes perpetrated on the American people. In this instance, both the Democrats and the Republicans share the same vision – *to stiff the American people,* and to give priority to illegal foreign nationals rather than American citizens. What happened to

America and Americans first? We discussed this topic in detail in Chapter 2 but we must think about how bad our politicians played this match so we can let them play someplace else other than as our representatives.

I hope this book as all others in the 4 Dummmies Patriotic series helps to wake up all Americans of all ages from the fog that has affected our brains. We have not changed but we have permitted our government to change. Our representatives and our government have changed so much that they have forgotten who we are and who we the people are supposed to be.

Nobody really expected a fundamental change in America from the guy who promised a fundamental change. Most of us thought he was talking about patching a pretty good system. Not so! He wants to eliminate America and create a communist socialist state in its stead. More and more Americans in year six think this fundamental change has nothing to do with making America better and it is not the change for which they voted.

Without using those exact words, our Constitution gives US a government *of the people, by the people, and for the people.* These exact words are used in the Declaration of Independence which was an operating precept when the Constitution was written.

The Bill of Rights specifically grants powers to the people that the government today wants to take away. The Constitution, of which the Bill of Rights is an add-on part— but integral to the purpose for sure, gives government just the powers that are specifically enumerated by the people and no more.

It is a shame that too many Americans have become lazy and we have permitted corrupt politicians to be reelected regardless of whether they represent US well or not. Shame on US!

Abraham Lincoln is the most famous historical figure to use this patriotic phrase. It was in his Gettysburg Address from November 19, 1863. For posterity, here is Lincoln's last paragraph. It is chilling:

"It is rather for us to be here dedicated to the great task remaining before us -- that from these honored dead we take increased devotion to that cause for which they gave the last full measure of devotion -- that we here highly resolve that these dead shall not have died in vain -- that this nation, under God, shall have a new birth of freedom -- and that government of the people, by the people, for the people, shall not perish from the earth."

If I ask you to do anything besides *pay attention* in this book, it is to reject the fundamental changes that are destined to bring in a much bigger government—bigger than the population at large. Big government doesn't work. Big agencies don't work. Big corporations don't work. Big doesn't work well at all, especially if you are one individual person looking for freedom and liberty.

Government has grown so big that we the people, who own the government according to a deed known as the Constitution, and some explicit notions such as *The Bill of Rights* can no longer sort through all the lies and the empty promises. Government has simply gotten too big and too powerful for regular citizens. Government has already become the biggest bully in America. Why should we let ig grow even bigger?

So, we must all help reduce the size of government for the people to ever matter again. We get our chances each election cycle. When we vote to favor corruption and the advocates of government growth, we get the government we deserve. They will be coming for us all!

If all Americans understood America, by knowing by heart the Bill of Rights and the Constitution, as many of us once learned in school, and if we were taught to respect America in our schools, instead of blaming America first for everything—we would not have to worry about being defeated from within.

In this way, if any American political party comes-by led by Democrats or Republicans, and it wants to change America into a Communist-Russian-like, or Communist-Chinese-like, or Naxi-German-like country, we will be better equipped to fire off a quick *nyet*, or a *mhai*, or simply, a hearty and guttural *nein*!

If you believe in any of the leftist progressive socialist philosophies and you also like your freedom, it might be a good time to visit the tombstone makers in your area and pick out a good one. In memoriam! You are gone!

Know your rights! Know the Bill of Rights!

Chapter 6   The Bill of Rights Says: Throws the Bums Out!

Write opinion letters and call your representatives

The purpose of this book as noted from the beginning is to help US all be better Americans by understanding the Bill of Rights, an essential ingredient of the US Constitution. At the same time, as an adjunct to a greater understanding of our rights, we learn a lot about America's founding. Most of us have heard parts of the Bill of Rights as parts of the US Constitution and if they have been presented properly, we more than likely, really like them. Who would say no to prosperity through liberty and freedom?

The Bill of Rights was actually an after-thought to the US Constitution—the defining document of our country. Doubtful Patriots, who examined the Constitution for approval, wrote that all powers and rights not explicitly given to the government were held by the people. So, let's say among other specific powers, the Constitution grants to the President, the Congress, and the Courts operating as the government the following powers / rights:

— To lay and collect import duties
— To pay the debts of the U.S. Government.
— To regulate commerce with foreign nations and Indian Tribes.
— To regulate commerce among the States.
— To regulate immigration.
— Etc.

As you can see, these are things that we all would expect government to do as well as a number of other specific tasks all laid out in the Constitution. As you read the Constitution in Appendix E, you will notice that certain rights for government are not included; such as:

— Killing Citizens.
— Preventing the people from assembling in groups of more than two.
— Demanding that the people shop only at government stores.
— Requiring men to shave
— Preventing the people from eating on Tuesday.
— Etc.

Only the rights specifically given to government in the Constitution are in government's purview. All other rights are reserved for the people. In other words, the people have all other powers and rights than those specifically given to government.

Since the Constitution gives almost all rights and powers to the people, there was disagreement among many of the founders and the citizens of the 1780's about the constitution outlining specifically all the rights of the people. There was a difference of opinion and the Bill of Rights ultimately arrived after the Constitution was ratified.

The majority of the Founders believed that by saying the people have all rights other than those reserved for government, as they wrote in The Constitution, and the government had only those rights specifically mentioned, that should have been enough. What more should we have needed?

To repeat, the Constitution as written from the beginning already provided all rights the people would ever put in a Bill of Rights, and the government was given its specific powers so it could function as a government.

Though this is not how it actually works, let's try this exercise to get a better understanding of our rights v. government rights.

Rather than saying the people have all rights not explicitly granted by the people to the government, let's suppose that the Founders tried to define every single right / power for all Americans. In this process, let's say they numbered the rights beginning with number 1.

Suppose when all the rights were listed and added to the Constitution, the number of rights was calculated to be, say, 437. What would happen if in trying to define the 437 rights, which in this scenario the Founders believed all Americans should possess, they forgot a right or just a part of right? Then what? What if this particular right's number just happened to be 93? Then what?

In this fictitious scenario to make our point, as noted, the Constitution as written provides not just for right number 93, but all rights from zero to 437 and beyond without any rights being specified. But, in this scenario, rather than global rights, the Constitution granted specific rights to the people. The people in this fictitious scenario did not have global rights. They had all rights defined from zero to 437 but none others and no parts that were forgotten and not specified.

Anything that would be a right of the people would have to be specified within the 437 defined rights or it would not be a right / power of the people. Government would have its listed powers and rights as well as discussed above but rights not listed for the people would be in the government column. Does that sound better than the people having all the rights except those they give to the government?

As you might suspect, there would be a problem when a missing right were needed, and the Constitution was finalized. So, what would happen when the people sought to have a right number 438, about which nobody ever would have conceived when the rights were originally numbered to 437? What if enough people were pro-government that they would not vote the people to have the additional rights or to have right # 93 amended to add the forgotten clause? It could create a big problem for the people. It gives government the greater hand over the people's hand.

So, what did the Founders do so that this would never happen?

1. The constitution specifically lists all of government's rights / powers.
2. All other rights are granted to the people.
3. A Bill of Rights was added to the Constitution for the people—though the Bill of rights is redundant since the Constitution already grants all rights not reserved for government to the people.
4. Since a new right is already granted by the Constitution, rights do not have to be granted specifically and were not often granted after the Bill of Rights was devised and ratified.
5. Despite this great compromise, only ten of the twelve rights proposed were ratified; and since that time, just seventeen changes were made to the constitution in the form of amendments—the same form in which the Bill of Rights were presented.

The Constitution and its 27 amendments including the Bill of Rights is the place to go to find out what America is all about! It is about the U.S. of A.—our nation. Our Country is what it is because its definition is embodied in its Constitution, which is America's most fundamental prized set of laws.

By the way, all amendments to the Constitution, especially the first ten known as the Bill of Rights, are in fact part of the Constitution. They are not adjuncts in fact to it; though they are in form. And thus, the Bill of Rights, the topic of this book is a major part of the Constitution. It is not a bunch of independent precepts brought forth to make us all feel better about life.

Our job, as Americans moving through life of course, is to learn what we can about our government (as defined by the Constitution—including the Bill of Rights et al.). In this endeavor, we should all pay attention that our Congressional representatives actually spend their time representing US according to the laws of the Founders, who, if they had their way, would never let US down.

When our representatives do not do the will of the people in-between elections we must remember that they represent US, not the government. We need to write letters to the editors of newspapers and other media, and write our Congressmen and Senators so they know they cannot snooker us, and so they know who is the boss—we the people.

If they don't listen, then we must do the honorable thing and write them even more letters, and letters to the editors of popular newspapers, and when they choose not to respond in our favor, or worse than that, not respond at all, we then must un-elect our leaders their next time out on the ballot.

Un-elect them! They would hate it!

Unfortunately for Americans, our representative in the Congress, the Supreme Court, and the Presidency is not

Jefferson Smith from the movie Mr. Smith Goes to Washington. His honor is impeccable. But, the honor of our representatives has become very questionable.

Do they represent US or do they represent themselves? Do they represent corporations or special interests? If our representatives are doing their jobs, why is our country screwed up so badly that it may be irreparable. When our country is handed over to non-citizens by our representatives, have they represented the citizens of the USA? When the President addresses the unescorted children from Central America and he tells them they are the future of America, what is he really telling our children?

Our representation has been getting progressively worse each year—not better. Over the past few years, especially from 2009 through 2015, with the healthcare debacle and open borders topping the list of domestic travails, it is clear that the voices of the people are not being heard in Washington, DC.

The government appears to be weakening our opportunity to survive as it cuts and cuts the health services that we need. How many of US want a corrupt government deciding if we live or die or what health services we can get or not get. Do you feel the same?

Just as Jefferson Smith in the Frank Capra classic movie, Mr. Smith Goes to Washington, found out, the corrupt purposes of elected officials is now in the open. It is to serve themselves by serving special interests.

In the sunlight of the day, therefore, the existing Congress—yes, both houses, must go. Not the institution of Congress, just the corrupt members who choose not to serve the people.

We must bid them sayonara. We must say adieu. We must sign off with a big adios. Our right to do this comes directly from the Constitution, not from the Bill of Rights—but it is a right of all Americans to un-elect the scoundrels that rip our country apart.

And when it comes time to elect our next President, and our next Congress; let's not forget to bring in an honest person who loves America as much as we do. If the mess we have today is not the President's intentions, and the President's direct fault, then whose fault, I might ask, is it? Might it be Stanley Laurel's or Oliver Hardy's—for it surely is a comedy!!

Surprise in today's email

Before I get to the surprise email in the heading, I got another surprise again today, while I was re-checking this book, hoping to clean it up for printing. Before I show you the picture and the remarks that I received, let me say that I was shopping at Malacari's, a great produce market in Wilkes-Barre PA, frequented by poorer people and smart shoppers. I am so glad Malacari's is in Wilkes-Barre.

When I was joking around with the checkout person and the person behind me; I admitted that I was unemployed (Most writers are unemployed until their works are sold.), but I did not say I was writing books hoping the big one would come in. Hah!

I said that I was thinking about running for President but that it seemed that everybody was so happy with the current President that I figured I should look someplace else for a job. I then said that everybody loves him so much, I would not have a chance anyway.

The Cashier stopped in her tracks and said: "that may have been a while ago but you should check again as it is not that way now." The lady behind her said that she "did not think anybody liked him anymore."

I have Democrat-loving can't do any wrong relatives in my family who are still doing well and they still are in love with the President. So, I figured the President was still doing OK. But, when these Jane Q Publics told me they were retired and collecting and still felt they had to work until they died, I started to think maybe you can't fool all of the people all of the time.

Wow! I was very surprised. As we examine the notions that come our way, isn't that why you are reading this book? Thank you to all the Americans ready to fight for American values. We need more of you today in our America! "Don't give up the ship." Keep firing until America wins.

You may know that about a year into the War of 1812, the first full scale war for the new America after the Revolution, Captain James Lawrence said these heroic words after being mortally wounded. It was in the engagement between his ship, the U.S. frigate Chesapeake, and the HMS Shannon on June 1, 1813. While the wounded Lawrence was being carried below, his duty for his ship and his love for America motivated him to order his officers: "Tell the men to fire faster! Don't give up the ship!"

Keep firing until America wins. Use the Bill of Rights, the Constitution, and all great American principles as your ammunition.

Chapter 7 The Declaration of Rights and Grievances

The First Document on the way to the American Revolution

Let's go back in time to right before the American Revolution. Before we wholesale study the Bill of Rights and the good it has done for America, let's take a trip back so that we all understand the many documents that came before this famous declaration of rights.

Ironically, long before the Bill of Rights, in fact, even before the outset of the Revolutionary War, one of the first documents on the way to the Declaration of Independence and The Constitution was the Declaration of Rights and Grievances, This is not the Bill of Rights, but it surely set the stage for American Independence.

This declaration was a product of the First Continental Congress. The colonists were upset with foreign rule from England because they were not given a real voice in the government. As an aside, unfortunately not much has changed for regular American citizens since that time.

As shown in its entirety in Appendix A, the Declaration of Rights and Grievances was the first formal request of the "United States" to England for a return to representative government. The colonists were seeking a return to a form of government as had originally been established by the Crown. The demands were not outlandish.

Though nothing close to a constitutional democracy, the Colonists under English rule enjoyed representation in the lower house of all of the colonial "state" governments.

There was no union of colonies or states at the time and had the English kept to themselves and not levied taxes directly on the colonists, Americans today would be much more interested if Camilla is really ever going to be the Queen.

With a careful reading of the Declaration of Rights and Grievances, one can get a quick sense of what the colonists wanted from the Crown. It was simply, "no taxation without representation," and all of the many positions this plea represented. As the thought of a revolution became more of a reality for the Patriots, independence and freedom and liberty became even more important than the tax burden.

This early declaration was the first major document of the new government of the United States, though it occurred at a time when the states were not actively seeking independence from the Crown.

The expressed purpose of the First Continental Congress held in 1774 was:

"That a Committee be appointed to state the rights of the Colonies in general, the several instances in which these rights are violated or infringed, and the means most proper to be pursued for obtaining a restoration of them."

The committee was constructed and the declaration was drafted and it was read on September 22nd and the draft of the grievances was read on the 24th. The members of the First Congress debated the drafts on October 12 and 13, and after a final draft was produced, it was agreed on Friday, October 14, 1774.

At this First Continental Congress, the delegates drafted several documents, and several drafts of documents, one of which was the document known as The Declaration of Rights and Grievances. This was the statement of American complaints agreed to on October 14, 1774.

The document was sent to King George III, to whom, at the time, many of the delegates remained loyal. It was not sent to Parliament since the delegates did not have the same level of loyalty to this body. Quite frankly, the document implored King George III to step in and rescue the colonies from the English Parliament.

The radical colonial delegates (aka Patriots) were critical of this particular Declaration because it continued to concede the right of Parliament to regulate colonial trade, a view that was losing favor in the mid-1770s. Many suggest that the actual cause of the American Revolution is found in this major historical document, which you can read in its entirety in Appendix A.

Chapter 8 The Articles of Association

Dear King George III

Several days after the signing and sending of the Declaration of Rights and Grievances to England, on October 20, 1774, the Congress passed the Articles of Association. They had been written during the same Congress. The Congress, by the way was the colonial Congress (First Continental Congress) and not the Congress of today. There was no House and no Senate for today's institutions were created by The US Constitution. The Constitution was about thirteen years away at this time in history.

Ironically in this day and age when progressive communists want to do away with the entire Constitution and they have a majority in the Senate and a President to help them in this traitorous cause, they have all received their power to exist—raison d 'etre—from the same Constitution that these dirty politicians in the Executive and Legislative branches hold in such disdain.

As with the Declaration of Rights and Grievances, the Articles of Association were also addressed to King George III. In essence, it was a formal agreement of the colonies themselves to work together as an association of states with common purpose. How King George would react to such demands was an interesting consideration. The colonist patriots were extremely brave men.

It was basically a union of protest and boycott as many of the articles that you will find in Appendix B, outlined the specifications that the colonists were to take regarding the export and import of goods.

When you read these articles in your own time, you can't help but notice the elegance and forethought in the draft. We are a fortunate lot indeed to have had such fine and capable, and yes, honorable men, representing America in our founding days.

Both the Declaration of Rights and Grievances as discussed in the prior chapter as well as the Articles of Association were prompted substantially by the Coercive Acts of Parliament enacted in the 1774 time frame. You can learn about all of these notions in other books within the 4 Dummmies Lets Go Publish! patriotic series but you can learn enough right here:

The Coercive Acts by Parliament included the following:

1. The Boston Port Act closed the port of Boston until damages from the Boston Tea Party were paid.

2. The Massachusetts Government Act restricted Massachusetts; democratic town meetings and turned the governor's council into an appointed body.

3. The Administration of Justice Act made British officials immune to criminal prosecution in Massachusetts.

4. The Quartering Act revisited from 1765, required colonists to house and quarter British troops on demand, including in their private homes as a last resort.

5. The Quebec Act. Though not technically part of the Coercive Acts, the colonists lumped a fifth act, known as the Quebec Act along with the four Coercive acts into a set of five that they referred to as "The Intolerable Acts." The Quebec Act extended freedom of worship to Catholics in

Canada, as well as granting Canadians the continuation of
their judicial system. Religious tolerance at the time was
not at its best. The mainly Protestant colonists did not look
kindly on the ability of Catholics to worship freely on their
borders.

When you have a chance, you should consider taking a look
at the Articles of Association in Appendix B as another major
document that helps define the American thought process
before America was ready to take up arms against England.

Because sometimes the long paragraphs of the founders,
though quite eloquent, put regular Americans to sleep. You
might consider checking out The Constitution 4 Dummmies
by LGP for a more cohesive treatment. Just as in this book I
have parsed some material to be more readable without
removing any words or meaning.

Another great source of information and also easy to read is
Sol Bloom's Epoch ... Story of the Constitution, which has
recently been re-mastered and refined and re-published by
Lets Go Publish! (LGP) www.bookhawkers.com

The Articles of Association are worth reading for sure.

History of the Articles of Association

God bless all the signers of the Articles of Association from
all the thirteen states of the first union. A brave lot they were
for sure. Where are brave Americans today in the mid period
from 2010 to 2020? It seems most are sleeping as our country
is in deep peril once again. The opposition is trying again to
beat us by disarming us. Keep your guns, please!

The Articles of Association were written while the colonies
hoped they could work out a deal with Britain so that
freedom did not have to come from war. As a side note, the

Brits knew the brave colonists were armed, and so even the mighty English walked gingerly in the colonies..

As you can see by reading the Articles of Association, this document calls on the colonies to stop importing goods from the British Isles beginning on December 1, 1774, if the Coercive Acts were not repealed.

You may enjoy checking out the coercive acts (aka to some as the Intolerable Acts). Though it is not the thrust of this book, by reading the very short historical synopsis in this chapter, presented above, you can get a sense of the items that were most upsetting to the colonists.

Should Britain fail to redress the colonists' grievances in a timely manner, this First Congress declared, then it would reconvene on May 10, 1775, and the colonies would cease to export goods to Britain on September 10, 1775. After proclaiming these measures, the First Continental Congress disbanded on October 26, 1774.

Have you ever seen America so decisive? For me, the closest time other than this was the Cuban Missile Crisis! Bravo JFK!

Colonial Americans loved America and could not believe the British were going to hurt any American who wanted real freedom. They understood why the British were upset by the _Boston Tea Party_ and other blatant acts of destruction of supposedly British property by American colonists. Yet, the colonists did not condone the British Acts, which eventually forced America's hand.

Still thinking that the Americans would do whatever was demanded, the British Parliament enacted the very nasty Coercive Acts, as previously discussed, much to the outrage of American Patriots, on March 28, 1774.

Historians know that the Coercive Acts were a series of four acts established by the British government. The aim of the legislation was to restore order from the Crown's perspective in <u>Massachusetts</u> and to punish Bostonians big-time for their "Tea Party."

The British saw this "Tea Party" as an emboldened act by the revolutionary-minded Sons of Liberty, who had boarded three British Tea Ships in Boston Harbor and dumped 342 crates of tea—nearly $1 million worth in today's money—into the water to protest the British Tea Act.

Since life had not improved for the British, who had become money-strapped, after initially backing off from its taxation impositions, they began to double down on the colonists. They continued to impose their will on the colonists.

Seeing it coming, Americans were ready for action. The Second Continental Congress began on May 10, 1775 and it went on until March 1, 1781. It was well in session during the Revolutionary War. Yes, the colonists, brave everyday folks as they were, took up arms against a super-power!

During the Revolutionary war, the Second Congress of the US continued, but its meeting location was moved from Philadelphia several times to other locations to protect the lives of the representatives.

Britain, as an adversary was not an easy foe with which to deal. The Americans needed to smarten up on the battlefield and so they looked for great generals. They found George Washington.

The English considered the American Revolution as tyranny, while the patriots in the colonies saw England's imposition of its strength upon the colonies as a tyrannical act that Americans could not tolerate.

The delegates from twelve of the thirteen original colonies gathered again in Philadelphia to discuss their next steps in dealing with England. This Second Congress met at the State House in Philadelphia (Now popularly known as Independence Hall) as the American Revolution had already begun in earnest with the shot heard round the world still ringing in their ears.

After major deliberations in Georgia, this last colony finally joined the Congress, dispatching delegates who arrived on July 20, 1775.

When the Second Continental Congress came together on May 10, 1775 it was, in effect, a reconvening of the First Continental Congress. The Colonies sent many of the same 56 delegates who attended the first meeting. They appointed the same president (Peyton Randolph) and secretary (Charles Thomson). Some now famous new arrivals to Congress included Benjamin Franklin of Pennsylvania and John Hancock of Massachusetts.

Peyton Randolph, the President of Congress, a very important person in Virginia Politics, was summoned back to Virginia unexpectedly to preside over the House of Burgesses within two weeks of the convening of the 2nd Congress. Virginia sent Thomas Jefferson, and other brave historical figure, to replace him. Jefferson arrived several weeks later.

Henry Middleton was elected as President of Congress to replace Randolph, but he declined. John Hancock was then elected President of the Congress on May 24, 1775. One might say that John Hancock was the 2nd President of the United States (Peyton Randolph was the first) at a time when the country operated without a Constitution. As you will see, the Constitution, which created a new government, created a new Congress and a lot more.

Massachusetts, which appears to have been the toughest state at the time, (turned wimpy over the years) much differently than the Massachusetts of today, had already organized the

Minutemen. This was a special militia that could be ready on a minute's notice.

Minutemen skirmished with British troops at Lexington and Concord. Meanwhile, other farmer-soldiers joined them outside Boston to fight for America. The militia was still engaged in Boston while the Congress was using its powers to formally establish the Massachusetts militia as the Continental Army of the United States with George Washington of Virginia as the top general.

The head of this army was known at the time as the Commander in Chief. And this general with the power won America its rights before America needed a Bill of Rights.

This marked another stage in the formation of the government of the US. The government would continue to evolve and after independence was gained, George Washington would again become Commander in Chief when he was elected First President of the United States.

Sixty-five representatives originally appointed to the Second Continental Congress by the legislatures of thirteen British North American colonies accomplished a body of work that is historical in nature. At the time, it formed the basis for the new government, ready to take on and defeat England.

The Declaration of Independence, with full text presented in Appendix C was the first well-known historical document produced by this Second Congress. The second was the Articles of Confederation, with full text shown in Appendix D.

All of this great documentation of the strife of the colonists in their relationship with Britain is put forth in all of these documents, the intent of which at the time was to make America free from England. The Articles of Confederation was the pre-cursor document to the United States Constitution, which is shown completely in Appendix E.

As noted previously, the Second Continental Congress was convened during the American Revolutionary War but prior to July 4, 1776. It served as the de facto U.S. national government as there was nothing else on the colonist side, as powerful. This Continental Congress assumed power and raised armies, directed strategy, appointed diplomats, and it made the US government a formal entity. Was it not amazing?

At the same time, this Congress of America's finest Founders, produced numerous important documents, including two of the most fundamental and historical documents to American freedom—*The Declaration of Independence and The Articles of Confederation*. Both of these documents led to the creation of the US Constitution in 1787.

Chapter 9 The US Declaration of Independence

By the Second Congress, July 4, 1776

You can see the agita rising as one document after another, showed the colonists placing simple requests from England for rights the colonists for years believed they already had.

Some dates, one can never forget. The Declaration of Independence was written by Thomas Jefferson, a relative newcomer and a real youngster, and it was put forth and approved for printing on July 4, 1776. It was a product of the Second Continental Congress. It did exactly what it purported to do in its title. It declared independence from Great Britain.

It was not Pennsylvania, or Massachusetts or Virginia that declared this independence and this is a key point. Instead, it was all of the thirteen colonies in unison, known to themselves as states at the time. They had chosen to assemble and join in a union to create a new federal government that would one day become known as the United States of America.

Once independence was declared, even though the fighting was underway, America began to legally operate fully independent of the Crown with its own government. Considering that the colonists were in revolt and war had commenced, it is an understatement to suggest that the colonists were not operating independently prior to the Declaration. The Declaration formalized their union of independence, and for those thinking that England still ruled the day, it solidified America as the major power.

If you are willing to fight for your statements, you can state anything. The colonists were ready to fight, and had in fact begun the fight!

The states were declared to be free and independent and "all political connection between them and the State of Great Britain, is and ought to be totally dissolved."

The formal title of the document ratified on July 4, 1776 is the "**Unanimous Declaration of the thirteen United States of America**," but to Americans it is known simply as the Declaration of Independence. This was the formal end of the thirteen colonies and the beginning of the United States of America!.

Declaration of Independence – Explanation and Additional Thoughts

In addition to declaring independence, this document gave justification for the separation from the Crown in sufficient detail that the King and Parliament could not misunderstand its purpose and from whence it came. Since the colonies were no more, historians consider this Declaration as the founding document of the United States of America. In his Gettysburg Address of 1863, at the beginning of his address, President Lincoln memorialized the founding of the United States in these words:

Four score and seven years ago our fathers brought forth on this continent, a new nation, conceived in liberty, and dedicated to the proposition that all men are created equal. And so, though some contest it, as the founding document; the Declaration of Independence still is in effect. Along with the essence of the Constitution and the ninth amendment (in the Bill of Rights) it gives the rights to the people, including rights not discovered at the time of the writing.

As we know from our knowledge of American History and its recount of the Revolutionary War, there were a number of battles until the Americans prevailed in the war with England. After the Declaration of Independence, the Second Continental Congress stayed in session, meeting periodically, passing laws and drafting other documents that ultimately would define the new nation as the United States of America.

The next major document in the formation of the government of the United States is known as The Articles of Confederation. These Articles served as the defining document of rules until a "more perfect union" was formed with the writing and the adoption of the US Constitution. Until The Constitution, the Articles of Confederation were the Law of the Land.

Chapter 10 US Articles of Confederation

Written and adopted by the Second Congress, November 15, 1777

While the Revolutionary War was still in progress, the Second Continental Congress adopted the Articles of Confederation, the first "constitution" of the United States, on November 15, 1777. However, ratification of the Articles of Confederation by all thirteen states did not occur until March 1, 1781.

Thus, it can be concluded that the whole revolution was prosecuted without benefit of a national set of laws. Having a Congress of the states in session filled in for the lack of a formal national body of law during this time. The Articles of Confederation were in "approval in process" status served as the model which Congress used to govern the new United States.

Just as the Declaration of Independence is short for a longer title, the "Articles of Confederation and Perpetual Union" has been shortened over time to be simply The Articles of Confederation. Some say that the Articles of Confederation represent the United States of America's first constitution. After the Second Continental Congress, the Articles established a "firm league of friendship," which is affirmed as a not too trivial perpetual union between and among the 13 about-to-be-united states.

After having been subjected to the wiles of the strong central government of the British prior to the War of Independence, these Articles reflect a sense of the wariness by the states of a government that would not provide them with their God-given rights.

The Articles are the agreed-upon remedy for the concerns of states' rights and for individual rights. Ever fearful that a government of the future (such as the current regime in the US or one hence) might not have the right measure of concern for our individual needs and rights if it were given too much power, and that abuses such as the Intolerable Acts, might again be the result, the Articles purposely established a guiding set of rules / laws, which in essence was a "constitution." It surely served the purposes of this fledgling government.

The full contents of the Articles of Confederation are shown in their original form in Appendix D. Next, in this chapter, we show the cover text; followed immediately by a facsimile of the original cover.

2

77

ARTICLES
OF
CONFEDERATION
AND
PERPETUAL UNION
BETWEEN
THE
STATES
OF
NEW HAMPSHIRE, MASSACHUSETTS-BAY RHODE ISLAND AND
PROVIDENCE PLANTATIONS, CONNECTICUT, NEW YORK, NEW
JERSEY, PENNSYLVANIA, DELAWARE, MARYLAND, VIRGINIA,
NORTH CAROLINA, SOUTH CAROLINA AND GEORGIA

WILLIAMSBURG:
Printed by Alexander Purdie

Now, here is how a copy of how the cover looked many years after it was printed:

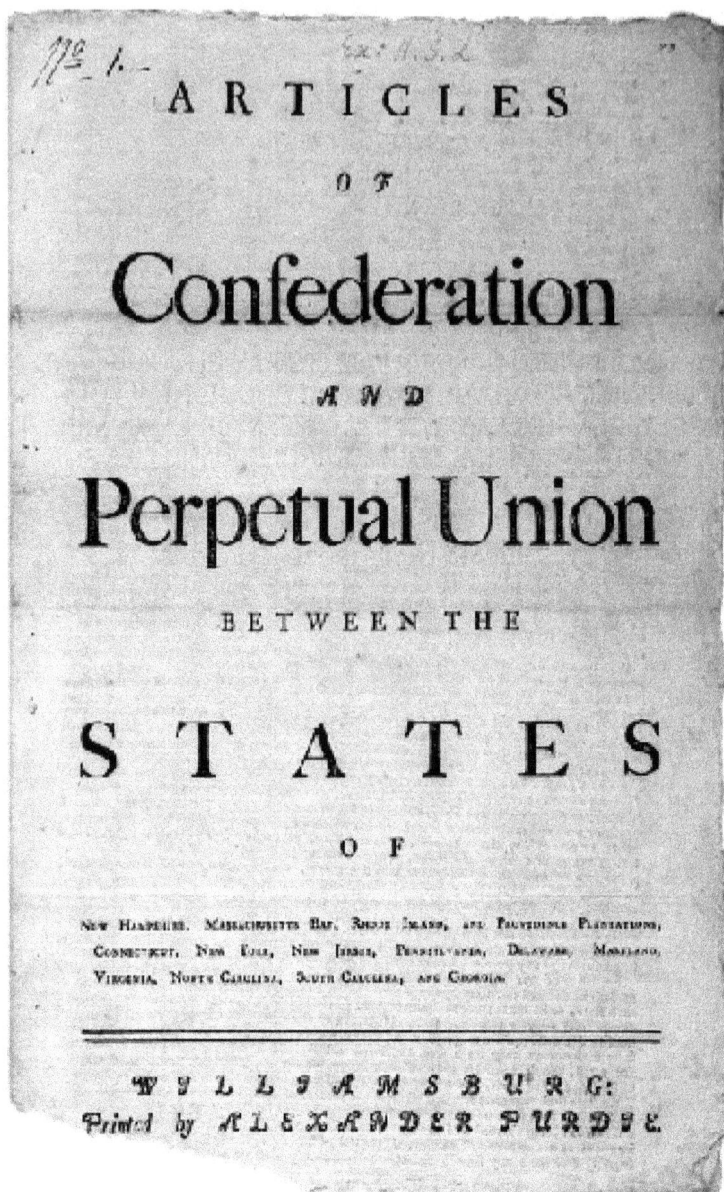

The complete text of the Articles is located in Appendix D. Explanations of The Articles of Confederation are available below and in chapter 10. Others descriptions are free online. Explanations also exist in other popular books such as

America 4 Dummmies! And The Constitution 4 Dummmies—available at www.bookhawkers.com.

Take a Look!

When analyzed correctly, the Articles of Confederation vested the largest share of power to the individual states. When the Constitution was built and later enacted, it reflected the same notion of states' rights and individual rights, as the Articles, and the last claimant on the rights list was the federal government in Washington D.C. The founders abhorred the notion of a strong central government such as a monarchy—like that of England's George III.

Under the Articles of Confederation, each of the states retained its "sovereignty, freedom, and independence." The preamble of the US Constitution drafted in 1787 and ratified later by the individual states one at a time, sets its purpose as "in order to form a more perfect union."

The founders of our government recognized that there were flaws in the Articles of Confederation that would more easily permit a tyranny to take place. And, so their best, "more perfect" work, the Constitution, was their way of correcting those flaws and correcting the notion of a constitutional representative democracy (aka, a Republic) for the United States.

There was a permanent institution called the Congress formed in the Articles as a national legislature comprised of representatives of the states. The Congress was responsible for conducting foreign affairs, declaring war or peace, maintaining an army and navy and a variety of other lesser functions.

The Articles did not call for the separation of powers with an executive, legislative, and judicial branch. The Articles did not permit the delegates to collect taxes, regulate interstate commerce and enforce laws. Under the Articles of Confederation these important functions could only be performed by the central government if the states agreed, and only for as long as the states agreed.

Though the Articles had these shortcomings, this historical and functional document provided the guidelines for the United States government and it was the only real law of the land until the Constitution was adopted and ratified.

Eventually, the shortcomings were addressed and this lead to the U.S. Constitution. The beauty of the Articles of Confederation was that they provided a workable framework during those years in which the 13 states were struggling to achieve their independent status from being one time colonies of England.

Considering that the Constitution itself is under fire today by those who would like it constructed in ways that were not intended by the Founding Fathers, from November 15, 1777, when adopted by the Congress, the Articles of Confederation did their job to keep the Country in good stead. Nothing in life worth having is easy.

On March1, 1781, the Articles became operational when the last of the thirteen states signed the document. The next happening was the work of the Framers to create the US Constitution.

Chapter 11 Why did the Confederation Fail?

The Articles were simply not good enough for America!

The Articles of Confederation, the direct predecessor of the Constitution had many great features but it was far from perfect. If the US was an island and would never face enemies, it would not have been as bad a structure but in reality it was not the body of law that would keep America safe and prosperous. And, so it needed to be changed.

The Confederation formed by the Articles brought no transformation of the government to satisfy the needs of a growing country. It did place on a legal foundation a structure that unfortunately needed rebuilding throughout. The main, and fatal, character of the government under the Articles is listed in Article II, "Each state retains its sovereignty, freedom, and independence, and every Power, Jurisdiction and right, which is not by this confederation expressly delegated to the United States." It was therefore a "league of friendship," with no teeth for enforcement.

Congress was the unique organ in which "each state shall have one vote." The vote of nine States in Congress was necessary to get anything done. The Articles contained many wise details which later were written into the Constitution; but this imperfect arrangement gave Congress no control and no power to raise money. A broke country, a weak country be!

The US central government could only make requisitions on the states (as it had done during the war), and then hope and pray that the states would give up the purse as requested. States were too autonomous and did not like giving the federal government any money and so they rarely did, and thus the central governing capability of the country was impaired and to be honest, it was categorically ineffective.

Congress was given control over foreign affairs but was given no means of making the states obey even the treaty requirements, or provide for the payment of the foreign debt. It was a government of responsibility without power. To foreign nations it was the united-states but to the states, it was merely what they chose to make it as the states held all the cards. Its dealing with the people was through States and not vice versa. It was tough to move this huge country into any action and it became even more difficult as the states grew.

During the Revolutionary War most of the States had adopted constitutions of their own. These provided for governments in separate departments—executive, legislative, and judicial—with bills of rights to protect the citizens especially from such evils as had caused the revolt against British control. They were based on the practices of colonial times and the current theories of government; and they gave control through the elective franchise over the lower house of legislature in all cases, as had been the rule of the colonies.

In the state governments that came about, there was usually an upper house, but the character of its election varied. The governor was chosen by the legislature. In only five cases, the four New England States and New York, consisted of a legislature with a chief executive elected by the people. The Articles of Confederation were, however, a thing apart from this movement, a concession to necessity rather than an inherent element of American polity.

Though it was successful in prosecuting the war, mainly because of the raw intelligence and persistence of George

Washington, it is small wonder that the Confederation was not a success. Congress recognized at once the financial need; but several efforts to get the States to amend the Articles, by adding the right to levy import duties, failed through lack of unanimous authorization. The Articles actually inhibited their being changed for the better.

Once the war ended, there was a collapse of moral fiber that seems always to follow a great clash of arms. Interest in the union steadily waned. Sates began to behave as independent countries. It became increasingly difficult to secure a quorum of attendance in Congress, and when there was a sufficiency of states represented, important measures were often blocked by the need to have nine state votes.

The time following the war was a period of economic distress. It was also a time of experimentation, of learning a hard lesson in government that would be remembered. The Continental Congress and Articles of Confederation not only remained a symbol of union; they also prepared the way for a better national government and left on hand agencies of government in good working order and various substantial acts of legislation. Among these were the ordinance for the government of the Northwest Territory, and that for the public-land survey. Yet, the tone was set that either the Confederation needed major improvement; or a new and more perfect form of government needed to be established. Plans were drawn up for both.

Chapter 12   The Road from the Confederation to the Constitution

The Virginia Plan

On May 29, 1787, the Constitutional Convention, convened for the purpose of improving the government, was ready to begin business. President Randolph "opened the main business" by introducing the "Virginia Plan." The intent was to either make the Articles of Confederation work or to scrap them. The Virginia Plan suggested scrapping most of the Articles and borrowing from the documentation in the Articles to fill in missing pieces of the Virginia Plan.

This plan, drafted by Madison, had been submitted by him in outline to Washington on April 16, 1787, and was later worked up in preliminary meetings of the Virginia delegation of seven members. It provided for apportioned representation, a legislature of two houses, the lower house (House) elected by the people, the upper one (Senate) was to have representatives (Senators) elected by the legislature in the states. .

The legislature was to have all the legislative powers of the Continental Congress, and also "to legislate in all cases to which the separate States are incompetent, or in which the harmony of the United States may be interrupted by the exercise of individual Legislation; to negative all laws passed by the several States, contravening in the opinion of the National Legislature the articles of Union; and to call forth the force of the Union against any member of the Union failing to fulfill its duty under the articles thereof."

"There was to be a national executive [President] and a national judiciary, with a council of revision formed out of them which should have a conditional veto on national legislation and also on the national legislature's shutting down any State acts. The central power was to guarantee a republican [not Republican Party) form of government and its territory to each State. Provisions for the admission of new States were included, and provisions for amendment without the assent of the National Legislature."

Also State officers were to be "bound by oath to support the articles of Union." This was the foundation for what was to become the Constitution of the United States. For its form it went back to practices of colonial and State governments; for its powers to the lessons of wartime and later experiences. It gave the central government coercive power over the State governments, while it guaranteed the continued existence of state governments. Since it made no provision for operation through the State governments, it contained the idea of direct action on the people, and the great "law of the land" principle was foreshadowed.

This was far more than a mere amendment of the Articles of Confederation and entirely contrary to the instructions given the delegates from Delaware. It was a large-State proposal.

Charles Pinckney also introduced a plan, the text of which is difficult to find in the archives, but probable extracts and an outline exist. Its general character was similar to the Virginia plan and its influence upon the final draft seems to have been considerable.

The next thirteen meetings were in committee of the whole upon the Virginia plan. To enforce the idea of this plan three resolutions, urged by Gouverneur Morris, were introduced declaring that a federal (that is, confederate) union of individual sovereigns was not sufficient; that a "national

Government ought to be established consisting of a supreme Legislative, Executive, & Judiciary."

The report which the committee of the whole made to the convention on June 13 was a development of the Virginia plan, with changes that gave the election of the upper house of the national legislature to the State legislatures; made the executive consist of a single individual, and gave him alone the provisional veto; and added a resolution for the ratification of the new Constitution by State conventions.

The Paterson Plan

During this period with the Articles forming the legitimacy of the US government, the rights of Americans were hanging in the balance. Meanwhile a number of the constitutional convention delegates (aka deputies) feared a strong central government. Their major concern was with preserving the power of the States. To this end, they devised an alternative plan, which was introduced by Paterson of New Jersey on June 15, 1787.

This merely added to Articles, the power for Congress to have the right to levy an impost and to regulate foreign and interstate commerce. It also authorized a plural executive and a federal judiciary. It made the acts of Congress and the treaties with foreign powers "the supreme law of the respective States so far forth as those Acts or Treaties shall relate to the said States or their Citizens," and it bound the judiciary of the States to proper observance. It also gave the national executive the right to call forth the power of the States to compel obedience by the States to such acts or treaties.

In essence, this plan left the character of Congress unchanged, with an equal State vote and choice of delegates by the State legislatures; it adopted the separation of national powers; and specified the supremacy of the Union within its sphere. There were thus concessions to the recognized need for a more efficient government, but they did not go very far. They merely patched up the old Articles; and not so well to heal them.

From this, a Compromise

There was always a battle between the large and small States with the powerful states wanting more say in the national government. To avoid a convention ending result, and no improvements to the government, the Connecticut deputies urged adoption of what was known as a Great Compromise. As hard as it may be to believe, out of the great conflict, which threatened to disrupt the convention, on July 16, 1787, emerged the adoption of this Great Compromise.

This gave representation based on population in the lower house, with the exclusive power to originate money bills in that house; but in the upper house an equal State vote. The special financial power of the lower house was also a provision in some of the State constitutions; but it was later practically nullified by giving the Senate the right of unrestricted amendment. During the discussion of this, a major division between the northern and southern States developed, due to the latter's demand to include their slave population in the delegate count.

As tough as it is for any of us to stomach now, remember slavery was legal back then. Importation of slaves remained legal for about thirty more years. As such, a big part of the compromise was to have slaves count towards the representation tally. The compromise dictated that three-fifths of the slaves should be counted as inhabitants.

This compromise, together with the election of the Senate by the State legislatures, did much to quiet the apprehension of the small-State party; but it was not a victory for those who wished to preserve the principles of the Articles of

Confederation, and when later each senator was given a separate vote, the idea of State representation in the upper house was weakened.

Yet, this compromise made it evident that sectional questions as well as those involving State's rights were to be met. This evidence was prophetic of future trouble

Law of the Land

The next important question was that of national control over State laws and actions. The delegates recognized its need but they had a problem with the notion of a direct veto and the idea of military enforcement of obedience was objectionable.

The plan noted above, as introduced by Paterson on June 15, 1787, suggested the remedy, which was adopted unanimously on July 17, 1787. This made the laws and treaties of the national government the supreme law, to which the State judiciaries were bound in their decisions.

Later the Constitution itself was added to the laws and treaties and the "supreme law of the States" was made the "supreme Law of the Land," which change might be considered as emphasizing the origin of the Constitution as the work of the whole-of the people-and not just of the States.

This great "Law of the Land" clause has been called the linchpin of the Constitution, since it effectively binds the parts into the whole. It has always been the chief basis upon which the courts have passed on the constitutionality of legislation, whether State or national. It embodies the principle of direct action by the national government upon the inhabitants, for the enactments of the Congress, the people's representatives, are laws directly binding upon the people themselves.

The New Government

The league of states embodied in the Articles of
Confederation was made by the States with minimal
adherence to the notion of a central power. The Constitution
was made by the People. The first three words of the
Constitution—"We the People"—declare by what authority
the United States of America is ruled.

Having won their liberty and independence by force of arms,
and having experienced distress and danger because of an
imperfect union, the people finally succeeded in forming the
more perfect Union which is ordained and established by the
Constitution.

The Constitution is a direct emanation from the people. It not
only prescribes the kind of government which shall hold the
States and the people together, but it limits and defines the
powers of the government itself. Neither the United States
Government nor the States can modify, enlarge, or restrict
their own powers.

They depend for their existence upon the people, who reserve
the right as set forth in the Declaration of Independence, to
alter or abolish their government. Until the people decide
otherwise, the United States is, in the noble phrase of Chief
Justice Chase, "an indissoluble Union of indestructible
States."

Many states today as in the 1860's with the secession and
slavery issues, are upset at the lawlessness of the government,
and are talking about the viability of secession, just like the
President's executive orders are lawless, secession would also
be lawless. However, if a President is lawless, and Congress
remains indifferent and permits the lawlessness, one would
think that implicitly the states would be authorized to secede
from a lawless government that itself does not adhere to the
Constitution.

Short of dissolving the entire government, a right which the people have possessed since they declared independence from England, secession may be a preferred method in a lawless land. This battle has yet to be fought but we are approaching a time in which the red and the blue states may very well choose to be on separate sides of two new governments.

If all was perfect, the union would be indissoluble by the Constitution, which also provides for the indestructibility of the States by guaranteeing to each State a republican form of government and equal suffrage in the Senate. Nobody today can say that government is operating as intended by the Founders.

Ironically, the model for major parts of our government including the major structural document—The Constitution—come from studying the British model. Yet, England has no written constitution. Its constitution or fundamental law is whatever Parliament says it is.

Therefore the judges of England enforce the laws of Parliament without any question as to their constitutionality. But under a written constitution creating a government with limited powers a nation must have some means of determining if laws are in accord with the basic principles set forth by the constitution.

The liberties enjoyed by Englishmen were wrested from the Crown. The American colonists claimed these liberties as their inheritance, and won by force of arms, the final right to them and to further ones which had been fostered by the conditions of the colonial governments.

"The government of the United States is not a concession to the people from someone higher up. It is the creation and the creature of the people themselves, as absolute sovereigns."

Who could have said this any better than Sol Bloom, the author of the 1937 best seller during the time of the Constitution's Sesquicentennial (150th anniversary)—"The Story of the Constitution." Let's Go Publish!, the publisher of this book, has re-mastered Sol Bloom's epoch, and it is available for purchase at www.bookhawkers.com

Chapter 13   The US Constitution

Introduction to the Constitution

The Articles of Confederation were admittedly an imperfect constitution for the newly formed union. To put this in proper perspective, would it have been possible for Bill Gates to have introduced Windows 8 in 1985 rather than Windows 1.0? That answer is a clear no.

Mr. Gates and Microsoft needed to go through all of the versions from Windows 1.0 to Windows 8 to learn what was needed in Windows 8. This is similar to how The Constitution is a better version of the first law of the land, the Articles of Confederation. Once there is a basis for something, it can be improved. As version 1.0, The Articles were well done but needed improvement. A "more perfect union" was necessary.

The additional features in the Constitution over the Articles of Confederation are substantial. In many ways it was like going from Windows 1.0 to Windows 98. Then, of course the Bill of Rights was like moving to Windows NT from 98. Now, add in the 17 other constitutional amendments, each a minor update to the Constitution, and we can ask ourselves in Microsoft parlance, "What version of the Constitution are we running today?

As an aside, besides the powers of government being separated, which items gave the government a higher probability for tyranny? George Washington described the biggest problem with the Articles of Confederation in just two words, "no money."

Under the Articles, the Federal government relied on the states for funding. Without the Constitution, America might really be the name of a large land mass with 48 countries, and two not so contiguous countries--Hawaii and Alaska. A country with no money could not survive over the long haul.

The barebones Constitution itself was far more perfect than the Articles of Confederation, just like Windows 98 was far more perfect than Windows 1.0. Microsoft could not immediately go to Windows 8 because nobody knew how any of the other previous versions would behave or be accepted, and all the subsequent iterations of Windows occurred from its use over time, and its technological successes and failings. So with the Constitution!

In many ways, our country grew the same way. The phrase "a more perfect union," in the Preamble of the Constitution notes the imperfections in a prior version and it introduces the rationale for the drawing of the Constitution from the Articles of Confederation.

We know from reading the prior chapter that the prior imperfect document was The Articles of Confederation. Bill Gates knew that the prior document to Windows was the last version of DOS without the Windows GUI. He knew he could make it better after he visited Xerox's Palo Alto Research Center and learned about GUI in the mid 1970's.

The U.S. Constitution (and its subsequent 27 amendments) mimics the idea of having a v3.1, V4.1.x, and V5.x.3. It has survived for over well over two-hundred years without many changes. This notion of a basis document and then perfections in subsequent versions testifies to the eventual almost perfection of the Constitution.

Like Windows, it went through multiple iterations to get to The Constitution. Back in 1787, it was built to be the basis of the constitutional representative democracy (Republic) of the

United States. If he were alive at the time, even Bill Gates would have approved.

From the National Archives:

http://www.archives.gov/national-archives-experience/charters/constitution.html

I like how this text from the national archives reads—so instead of trying to rephrase this, I have included it below to explain the purpose of the work behind the Constitution. We have heard this before in this book, and so it should ring quite familiar.

> *"The Federal Convention convened in the State House (Independence Hall) in Philadelphia on May 14, 1787, to revise the Articles of Confederation. Because the delegations from only two states were at first present, the members adjourned from day to day until a quorum of seven states was obtained on May 25. [I would bet the adjournments took the quorum-less participants to Philadelphia's historic City Tavern, a fine place even today to libate.] Through discussion and debate it became clear by mid-June that, rather than amend the existing Articles, the Convention would draft an entirely new frame of government.*

The City Tavern, Philadelphia, PA

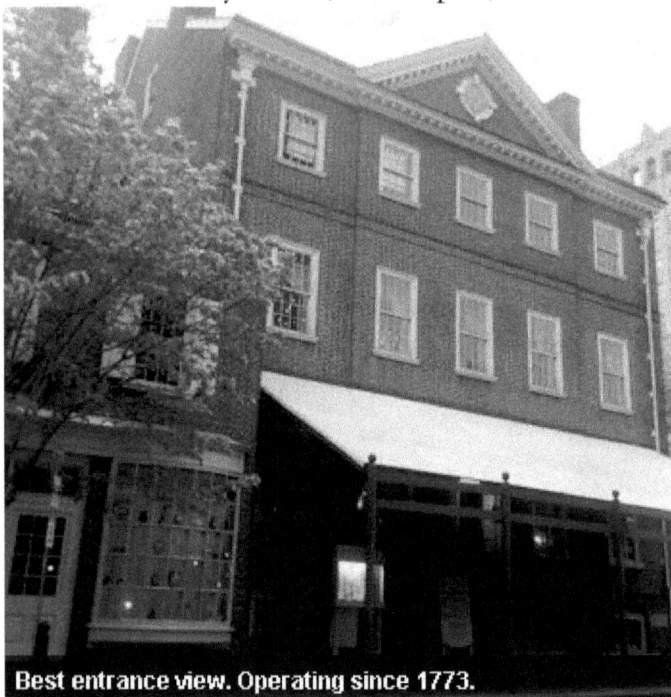

Best entrance view. Operating since 1773.

"All through the summer, in closed sessions, the delegates debated, and redrafted the articles of the new Constitution. Among the chief points at issue were how much power to allow the central government, how many representatives in Congress to allow each state, and how these representatives should be elected--directly by the people or by the state legislators. The work of many minds, the Constitution stands as a model of cooperative statesmanship and the art of compromise."

The Law of the Land

As noted previously, since 1787, the Constitution of the United States has comprised the primary law of the U.S. Federal Government. In simple terms it is the law of the land and all other laws must conform to the statutes contained within this original document and its amendments, from the Bill of Rights to Amendment # 27.

This law also describes the three chief branches of the Federal Government and their jurisdictions as well as the separation of the powers. It also gives the nation the ability to levy taxes, though an income tax was not permitted in the Constitution on people or corporations. Let's take a break and look more closely at the amendment. We'll be back soon.

Ironically, and quite smartly, there was no income tax provision in The Constitution. The Founders did not want a personal or corporate income tax mainly because it might be apportioned so that certain states paid more than others to the central government.

The people in the early twentieth century for their own reasons voted to ratify the Sixteenth amendment to the Constitution. This gave the Congress the right to tax them and US, and corporations at a personal level. Dum, Dumm, Dummm, and Dummmer must have been the lawyers representing the people in the campaign for passage of this terrible amendment. In the passage of this law, there was both chicanery and a lot more irony.

As hard as it may be to believe, the Sixteenth Amendment (which gave the American people the misery of confiscatory income taxes) was a trick. It never was supposed to have passed. Good people representing good people would never have permitted it.

It was introduced by the Republicans as part of a political scheme to fake-out the Democrats from a tax increase bill that would have passed but could never have been enforced because it would be unconstitutional. But, the trick backfired.

As previously noted, the Founding Fathers had rejected income taxes (as well as any other direct taxes) in the Constitution unless they were apportioned to each state according to population.

The politicians in the US Senate in the early 1900s passed a bill to institute the Sixteenth Amendment permitting such direct taxation in violation of the Founder's intentions. They wanted more largesse to distribute to assure their elections.

The people of course would have to ratify such an amendment if it passed Congress. It surprisingly passed unanimously 77-0 in the Senate! The House also approved it by another large margin, 318-14. Nobody was thinking, including the people in the states!

It was then sent to the states for ratification. State after state ratified this "soak the rich" amendment, thinking it would not affect them until it went into full force and effect on February 12, 1913. The people voted to tax the rich but just about everybody has been taxed ever since. You can never outfox a foxy politician. President Wilson was the best at politics and communism and progressivism, but he was not a very good leader in other ways.

In the Economic Policy Journal in April 2012, David, a blogger, called it right with his opinion of many Americans. His explanation, which is quoted below is that Americans would not vote for somebody, even Ron Paul who they truly believe would eliminate the income tax on everybody, because they think the rich should pay all the taxes and they should pay none. David sees it as a matter of class envy and offers a bleak outlook on the chances of it getting better until people wake up. Let's not be David, please. See what he has to say:

"Americans are envious and covetous of the wealth of others. They don't want freedom. They like a government that will do things to them, so long as the resulting chains appear to be gold plated. They like politicians that stir up class envy. Humans by nature are slaves. They don't yearn to be free, responsible, independent people. Until this wholly selfish and self-centered people awaken from their slumber; and learn to hate their slavery to government, until the iron of their chains eats into their soul, things are going to get worse."

The fact that Americans are beginning to get upset is a good sign. More and more people, like you, the reader, will be looking to learn about their rights and then I predict they will come after government with a vengeance. The times when politicians could survive despite their malfeasance in office are about to end because the people are about to end it. Thank you for reading this book.

I like to repeat to make a point. The fact that good citizens such as you are reading a book about the Bill of Rights is another good sign. I think this will all turn around with the help of some good leaders. That means we Americans must do our best to kick every federal politician (representative) out of office and replace them with good people as soon as we can. Then we take our battle to the state capitals, and then the cities. Finally, America will be run by the people again.

Back to the Constitution

In addition to permitting all but direct taxation, The Constitution lays out the basic rights of citizens of the United States. The Constitution of the United States is the oldest federal constitution in existence in the world, and it was framed by a convention of delegates from twelve of the thirteen original states in Philadelphia in May 1787.

The Constitution is the landmark legal document of the United States and all other laws are tested against its specifications. Many other constitutions, such as the Constitution of Mexico, for example are based on this work.

The text of the entire Constitution is included in Appendix E. The Bill of Rights (first ten amendments) and the other 17 amendments are described in detail in subsequent chapters as well as in Appendix F. Those Amendments that were submitted but not passed or ratified are shown in Appendix G.

To give the reader an appreciation or a reminder of just how significant the Articles and the Amendments of this document really are, I am including the entire text known as the Constitution in Appendix E.

The Constitution is a free document for anybody to record and retransmit in any form. It is over two hundred twenty-five years old. It makes America, America. It is available in this book, (Appendix E) and on the Internet from many sources and some sources are better than others.

Summary of the US Constitution

Explanation / Summary of Article I of the US Constitution:

Article I: The Legislative Branch consists of 10 sections and defines:

1. All Legislative powers,
2. Composition of the House of Representatives,
3. Composition of the Senate
4. Holding Elections,
5. Congress sets its own rules by House,
6. Compensation for Senators,
7. Revenue Bills originate in House,
8. Congress can lay and collect taxes,
9. States' rights and taxes,
10. State treaties.

Note: Article I, Section 9, Clause 8 of the Constitution is of particular interest to this writer. In later chapters we lightly discuss the automatic conferring of the title, the *Honorable*. Please look at what the founding fathers thought of such titles:

For your convenience this is provided here and in its proper place:

Section 9 Clause 8: *No Title of Nobility shall be granted by the United States: And no Person holding any Office of Profit or Trust under them, shall, without the Consent of the Congress, accept of any present, Emolument, Office, or Title, of any kind whatever, from any King, Prince, or foreign State.*

Article II: The Executive Branch: Consists of 4 sections and defines:

(1) Executive Power and President, (2) President as Commander in Chief, (3) State of the Union & Information Requirements, (4) Rules of Executive Branch impeachment

Article III: The Judicial Branch: Consists of 3 sections and defines:

(1) Judicial Power, (2) Laws and Trial by Jury, (3) Treason

Article IV: Relations Between States: Consists of 4 sections and defines:

(1)Faith and Credit of State Laws, (2) Privileges apply to all in all states, (3) New States May be Admitted to the Union, (4) Federal guarantee to defend states.

Article V: The Amendment Process: Consists of 1 section and defines the amendment process for adding / deleting to/from the Constitution.

Article VI: General Provisions, Supremacy of the Constitution: Consists of 1 section and defines the debt process and the requirement to support the Constitution

Article VII: Ratification Process: Consists of 1 section and it outlines the process for ratifying the Constitution.

End of Constitution summary. The full text of the US Constitution is included in Appendix E.

Chapter 14 Before the Constitution and the Bill of Rights

They were tough; knew their rights & would not be pushed around

Americans have believed in their rights and freedoms and liberties for many years—long before the Constitution. In fact the notion of rights goes far back into Colonial America when British subjects outnumbered all other immigrants and were under British dominion. These colonists brought with them the traditions of British' rights, liberties, and immunities, British laws and customs, and the English language to boot.

The notion of privileges and immunities is not something that we hear about every day or something we use in everyday language. Privileges and Immunities for our purposes in this book are concepts contained in the U.S. Constitution that place the citizens of each state on an equal basis with citizens of all other states in respect to advantages resulting from citizenship in those states and citizenship in the United States.

The privileges and immunities of which we speak are protected under Article IV of the Constitution and they include the right to receive protection from state government; the right to acquire and possess all kinds of property; the right to travel through or reside in any state for purposes of trade, agriculture, or professional endeavors; the right to claim the benefit of the writ of Habeas Corpus; the right to sue and defend actions in court; and the right to receive the same tax treatment as that of the citizens of the taxing state. As you will see, these rights are not the same exact rights that we find in the Bill of Rights.

Most countries from time immemorial have been run by absolutists and dictators. An absolute monarch for example, is one who wields unrestricted political and executive power over the sovereign state and its people. Over time, in more enlightened countries such as England, the people have been able to bargain for more rights from the government. But, this is not the case in most absolutist countries.

During the 1700s, for example, the England that lorded over the colonists was governed under a mixed "semi-constitution," made up of the monarch, the House of Lords and the House of Commons. These two houses were collectively known as Parliament. This type of government in the 1700s for England was the result of events that occurred in the previous century, when King Charles I was executed and England briefly became a republic.

Eventually the monarchy was restored in 1660. Charles II became king, but the new parliament held many more powers than had been the case during Charles I's reign. In other words, the English people gained additional rights.

And, so we can say that it was centuries of struggle that had won for Englishmen many guaranties of rights, liberties, and immunities. English common law was fairly established when the colonies were begun. Some rights and immunities, which had been enjoyed from time immemorial by the English, were reduced to writing in the Magna Charta, which was squeezed out of King John by the barons of England at Runnymede way back in 1215. Rights are not something foreign to the English people.

Other individual rights in England were formally guaranteed in writing, notably the Bill of Rights under William and Mary in 1689. The system of "constitutional government" safeguarded by a parliament elected by the people was well established when the first colonial charter was granted.

It helps to note that the liberties and rights of Britons were concessions from kings who ruled as by divine right and who originally possessed all authority. These concessions, and continual concessions over time, underlie the monarchical system to this day.

Colonial Americans wanted English rights

The colonies, beginning with Virginia and New England, were settled under charters granted by the King of England. These grants made large reservations of royal privilege and relatively small concessions to the emigrants. Broadly speaking, the colonists did not at first enjoy civil and political liberties as they were known in England.

Protests against denial of privileges enjoyed by British freemen were made in Virginia as early as 1612. Gradually the colonies were given larger powers of government, always provided that colonial laws should be in conformity to the laws of England and that allegiance to the Crown should be acknowledged.

The colonial period of the people who became Americans technically can be defined as from 1492 to 1788, which was the year in which the US Constitution was ratified. It therefore established the USA as we now know it. The period of English dominance in the Colonies began much later than 1492, and lasted about 170 years. The colonists therefore had abundant experience during this period in various forms of government under British authority, and they well knew a right from a prohibition.

In some respects eventually the colonists achieved substantial home rule and they enjoyed many individual liberties equal to those enjoyed by the English in England. But in matters of trade, the British government persisted in sacrificing the rights of the colonies to the advantage of Britain. This situation developed endless friction, complaint, and evasion of the British regulations. Americans, from England, or from elsewhere, resented the use of their success to fund the Crown for a perception of no value received.

When the colonists revolted against England, it was not as much because they had no rights as that they were treated as step-children, and a source of booty for England. The colonists were enraged at the treatment and would sacrifice life and limb to gain back their perception of freedom. As we all know, and thank the Lord for providing, America prevailed in the Revolution and eventually drafted its own Constitution.

As of 2016, only twenty-seven amendments have been attached to the Constitution. We call the first ten of these amendments, the Bill of Rights. As previously discussed in this book, the Bill of Rights did not come without controversy. However, unlike today's me-first politicians, the founders cared enough to work to make sure they got the best deal for Americans for all time to come.

The conventions of several States consented to ratify the Constitution only after they became satisfied that the Bill of Rights would be made an important part of it. Memorializing this achievement, many are aware that on March 18, 1936, in an eloquent address to the United States Senate, dealing specifically with the fourth and fifth amendments, Senator Ashurst of Arizona gave a vivid picture of the genesis of the Bill of Rights.

This is a fitting for our detailed discussion in the next several chapters of The Bill of Rights 4 Dummmies. This speech is extracted from Sol Bloom's ... Epoch Story of the Constitution a work published by Let's Go Publish!— available online at www.bookhawkers.com.

Referring to the ancient right expressed in the phrase, "Every man's house is his castle," Mr. Ashurst said:

"A gentleman calling upon me once asked, 'Did you ever read Lord Coke's famous maxim in Semayne's case?' to wit, 'The house of every one is to him as his castle and fortress, as well for his defense against injury and violence as for his repose.' I said, 'I am familiar with Coke, but that was law 1,000 years before my Lord Coke adorned the bench. ' "

Senator Ashurst added:

"The makers of our Federal Constitution and the framers of the first 10 amendments were never tired of quoting the immortal words of the elder Pitt, used in his speech on The Excise:

" 'The poorest man may in his cottage bid defiance to all the force of the Crown. It may be frail; its roof may shake; the wind may blow through it; the storms may enter; the rain may enter-but the King of England cannot enter. All his forces dare not cross the threshold of the ruined tenement.'

"When the ratification of the Federal Constitution was pending before the Virginia convention, called to pass upon that momentous question, Virginia was a pivotal State—a diamond pivot—on which mighty events turned. Patrick Henry, whom Lord Byron said was 'the forest-born Demosthenes who shook the Phillip of the seas,' was a delegate to the Virginia convention; and although the proposed Federal Constitution had come forth with the sanction of the revered name of General Washington and therefore justly carried with it the vast prestige which the name of Washington could not fail to
attach to any proposition, Patrick Henry did not approve the Constitution and, to use his own expression, he was 'most awfully alarmed,' as he considered the document to be threatening to the liberties of his country—amongst other

reasons because it lacked a bill of rights—and Mr. Henry challenged the view of Mr. James Madison, he of the superb intellect; Mr. Henry challenged the Wythes, the Pendletons, and the Innesses, and that splendid galaxy of scholars and statesmen who enriched the annals not only of Virginia but all America; and he demanded to know why a Bill of Rights, guaranteeing the privileges and immunities of the citizen, had been omitted from the Federal Constitution."

Bravo Patrick Henry! We all know that this fine American was surely a patriot! Great people take a toll, most often positive, on the efforts of the unsure. Patrick Henry was as sure of his convictions and his words as those who fought him were not so sure of theirs. The opposition could not figure out why Henry was wrong, and consequently, since it was all good people in the debate, giving in was not so hard—even for other great patriots among the Founders.

The Virginia State convention, after a prolonged debate, was able to ratify the Federal Constitution by a majority of only 10 votes, so ably did Patrick Henry argue against it because it did not contain the Bill of Rights, which English liberty had affirmed for centuries.

James Madison pledged his word that at the earliest opportunity he would use his energy toward placing into the Federal Constitution the requisite amendments guaranteeing the citizens' rights, privileges, and immunities, and as soon as the Virginia convention had finished the work of ratification it adopted resolutions expressing its desire for the Bill of Rights, as demanded by Patrick Henry. Madison was true to his word.

These resolutions were forwarded to the governors of the various States, and as far as men could be bound in faith and honor, as far as men could be bound in statesmanship and in politics, the amendments guaranteeing the citizen's individual rights and his liberties were by common consent agreed to, and it was generally understood that these amendments would be proposed to the States by the First Congress.

The Constitution therefore was ratified first without the Bill of Rights. It was not possible to amend the constitution as prescribed in the Constitution with first there being a Constitution. The Constitution established the Congress and the presidency, and the Courts system.

The first bill to be considered by the First Congress under the Constitution was quite naturally a bill to raise revenue to pay the many expenses of the government which had already incurred. But, as expected, the next had to do with rights! On July 21, 1789, James Madison, who was a Member of the House, arose and asked the House 'to indulge him in further consideration of amendments to the Constitution.'

Madison pointed out that the faith and honor of Congress were pledged; that the faith and honor of public men everywhere were pledged to amendments securing to the citizens such guaranties as were comprehended within the first ratified 10 amendments.

"The Bill of Rights amendments were then proposed to the States, including of course the fourth and fifth, and were ratified within 2 years and 3 months. Thereafter, as far as Americans are concerned, and as far as the Constitution itself is concerned, they were and are a part and parcel of the original Constitution, as much so as if they were signed on the 17th of September, 1787, when the main instrument itself was signed."

The ten amendments constituting the Bill of Rights are restrictions upon national power. As we see today in America, the elusive notion of the people possessing all power on all issues regarding powers not granted specifically to the Federal Government, falls apart when a president simply does not buy that argument and with a corrupt press in his tank, convinces half of the American people that he is above the law—and that it is perceived by the press and an apparent majority that it is OK! That, my dear readers is why some people right books about writes.

The rights and immunities enumerated in the Bill of Rights were already in existence with the ratification of the Constitution but they were not explicit. The people had all their rights and liberties after the war even before they created the Constitution. The Constitution was established to assure these rights, among other purposes, to make the people's liberties secure against oppression by the government, which they were in the process of setting up.

The Bill of Rights was created to make the people more comfortable with the notion that the government would be controlled, by the people, and would operate for the people, and be operated of the people. Let's now take a quick ride through the essence of each of the first ten rights outlined in the Bill of Rights. Americans need every one of these regardless of executive orders to the contrary.

I.

The First Amendment, related to religion, free speech, right of assembly and petition, debars Congress from establishing a religion or prohibiting free exercise of religion, or abridging the freedom of speech or of the press, or the right of the people peaceably to assemble and to petition the Government for a redress of grievances.

Efforts to check the evil practices of lobbying for most of the 20th century and beyond have been checked when they sought to abridge the right of petition; but freedom of speech and of the press does not permit the publication of libels, blasphemous or other indecent articles, or other publications injurious to morals or private reputation.

A publisher is subject to punishment for contempt if his articles tend to obstruct the administration of justice. The right of free speech does not give immunity for every possible use of language.

II.

The Second Amendment confers upon the people the right to bear arms. It also forbids Congress from infringing upon that right.

III.

The Third Amendment protects the people against military intrusion in their homes. In the colonial period, there were times when via the English quartering act, Americans citizens were forced to make their homes available to British Soldiers.

IV.

The Fourth Amendment guarantees the security of the people in their persons, houses, papers, and effects against unreasonable searches and seizures. Almost up to the hour of the evolution the American people had suffered from such injuries at the hands of the British government; and they were determined that their own government should not have power to invade their privacy by "writs of assistance," as general search-warrants were called. John Adams, speaking of James Otis' heroic protest against that practice, declared,   "The child Independence was born on that occasion."

V.

The Fifth Amendment protects the citizen against double jeopardy, self-incrimination, deprivation of life, liberty, or property without due process of law, and loss of property taken for public use. Far-reaching decisions by the courts have protected the citizen under these clauses.

VI.

The Sixth Amendment secures the right of trial by jury, and other rights while under criminal trial. The prohibitions are laid upon Congress, and not upon the States.

VII.

The Seventh Amendment guarantees the rights of citizens in civil trials.

VIII.

The Eighth Amendment prohibits excessive bail and fines, and cruel and unusual punishment. The Supreme Court will interfere with the action of State courts if they impose fines which amount to a deprivation of property without due process of law, but will do this under the Fourteenth Amendment.

IX.

The Ninth Amendment provides that the enumeration of certain rights shall not be construed to deny or disparage other rights retained by the people. "This amendment," said the Supreme Court (Livingston v. Moore, 7 Pet. 551) "indicates that the Federal Constitution is but a delegation of powers, which powers, together with the implied powers, constitute all that the Federal Government has or may presume to exercise." The people retain many rights which are not enumerated, and the Government has no power to interfere with these rights.

X.

The Tenth Amendment is vitally important in preserving the powers of the States and the people against encroachment by Congress [and the president]. It retains to the States or the people all powers not delegated to the United States nor prohibited to the States by the Constitution. In observance of this amendment the Supreme Court has halted attempts to invade the powers of the States, notably in the matter of commerce (there have been numerous examples of this in recent years).

The power of the States to regulate matters of internal police applies not only to the health. morals, and safety of the public, but also to whatever promotes the public peace, comfort, and convenience. State laws enacted under this power may be harsh and oppressive without violating the Constitution, but the restrictions of the Fourteenth Amendment apply.

Chapter 15 Amendments Post Bill of Rights

Amendments 11 to 27

The good news for all Americans is that the Constitution implicitly grants rights to the people, who are not necessarily properly served by government. But the idea of explicitly noting the people's basic rights to life, a.k.a. the people's rights and the powers of the people is a great idea.

All twenty-seven amendments (Including one to ten – the Bill of Rights) to the Constitution are provided in Appendix F with summaries in this Chapter and the last.

Let's now take a quick ride through the essence of each of the seventeen amendments ratified one at a time after the Bill of Rights. Each of these rights can be seen as a different release of the Constitution, and in few cases, perhaps a different version. If this were Windows, perhaps it would be version 10 or perhaps even version 20.

XI.

The Eleventh Amendment exempts a State from suit by a citizen of another State or a foreigner. It does not deprive the Supreme Court of jurisdiction over suits between States. Nor does it prevent suits against individuals holding official positions under a State, to prevent their committing wrong or trespass under sanction of an unconstitutional statute.

XII.

The Twelfth Amendment was declared in effect September 25, 1804, after a deadlock in the election of a President of the United States. Under the original electoral provision the elector voted "for two Persons," without designating either for President or Vice President. Jefferson and Burr received an equal number of votes in the election of 1800, and 35 ballots were taken in the House of Representatives before the choice fell to Jefferson. The amendment requires electors to vote separately for President and Vice President.

XIII.

The Thirteenth Amendment abolishes slavery. It differs from the first ten amendments in that it restricts the power of the States as well as that of the national government. It removed legal doubt as to the validity of the Emancipation Proclamation.

The drafting of men for military service does not violate this amendment, since a soldier is not a slave; and the contract of a seaman does not violate the spirit of the amendment.

An act of Congress declaring that no distinction should be made between race or color in denying admission to accommodations and privileges in inns, public conveyances and theaters was held unconstitutional [at this time], because denial of these privileges does not subject any person to any form of servitude or fasten upon him any badge of slavery.

XIV.

The Fourteenth Amendment puts beyond doubt that all persons, white or black, whether former slaves or not, born or naturalized, and owing no allegiance to any foreign power, are citizens of the United States and of the State in which they reside.

The States are prohibited from abridging the immunities of citizens, and from depriving any person of life liberty, or property, without due process of law, or denying to any person equal protection of the laws.

A State law fixing the employment of mine workers at eight hours per day does not contravene the amendment. Statutes regulating the manufacture and sale of goods are within the amendment.

The amendment does not add to constitutional privileges and immunities. The right of suffrage is not one of these rights.

But, soon it would be as the nation was able to address its shortcomings.

XV.

The Fifteenth Amendment provides that the right of citizens to vote shall not be denied or abridged on account of race, color, or previous condition of servitude. It does not confer upon any one the right to vote.

The power to determine qualifications of voters is left to the States; but they may not confine the voting right to white persons. *Yes, there is a period there.*

XVI.

The Sixteenth Amendment gives Congress power to tax incomes, from whatever source derived, without apportionment among the several States. This is not an extension of the taxing power, but it removes all occasion for an apportionment among the States of taxes laid upon incomes. The salaries of United States judges are not subject to tax, since the Constitution provides that they shall not be diminished.

With the sixteenth amendment, Congress and the president were permitted to demand all Americans pay for the government through their incomes.

XVII.

The Seventeenth Amendment changes the mode of election of United States Senators. Contests in State legislatures over election of senators had caused great dissatisfaction, and it was believed that election by the people would be an improvement.

Some of us still think it is a good idea for the states to elect Senators. In that way, when a Senator chooses to represent the Senator, the state, by direction of the people can call back the Senator and appoint one who better represents the people.

From my perspective this may have originally appeared to be a good amendment but it hurt the people. The people are stuck with a bad senator now for six years. What a shame.

XVIII.

The Eighteenth Amendment provided for prohibition of the manufacture, sale, transportation, importation, and exportation of intoxicating liquors for beverage purposes. Congress and the States were given concurrent power to enforce the amendment. Elliott Ness is the only person who seemed to take the law seriously.

The amendment became effective January 16, 1920. It proved to be unsatisfactory, for many reasons. Confusion arose because of the division of police powers. Enforcement by the national government was impossible. It was urged that this amendment was in conflict with the fifth, by taking property without due process of law. What would be next, outlawing 16-oz soft drinks in NYC?

It conflicted with the provision which makes the acts of
Congress the supreme law of the land. Personal liberty, it
was claimed, was abridged. On this point the Supreme
Court said (Corneli v. Moore, 267 Fed. 456):

"It may be a matter of regret that age-old provisions
making for the liberty of action of the citizen have been
encroached upon, and to a degree whittled away; but this
is not a matter wherein the courts may relieve. It is a
political question and not a judicial one."

In other words, the Supreme Court chose not to go along
with regular Joe's. They do not always get it right!

After 13 years of trial, with increasing confusion,
dissatisfaction, and expense, the Eighteenth Amendment
was repealed by the Twenty-first Amendment, which
became effective December 5, 1933. Prohibition was gone
and Ness, God love him, hopefully retired on a great
pension, which unfortunately today could not be afforded
by the people.

XIX.

The Nineteenth Amendment provides that the right of
United States citizens to vote shall not be denied or
abridged by the United States or any State on account of
sex. It was declared adopted August 26, 1920. The first
proposal to amend the Constitution to provide for woman
suffrage was offered by Senator Sargent, of California, in
1878, at the request of Miss Susan B. Anthony.

Fifteen States had granted complete suffrage to women
before the amendment was adopted, and in all but nine of
the rest they had partial suffrage. A woman was elected to
the House of Representatives from Montana in 1916.
Women first voted on a national scale in the presidential
election of 1920, and apparently their total vote was about

6,000,000. It is believed that at least 12,000,000 women voted in 1932.

When we think of the dummmness that has been so prevalent in our government throughout time, most of the time, it was because of the perception of popular thinking, not because of animus. Blacks were freed by Abraham Lincoln along with a whole lot of white guys who never held anybody, white or black, as a slave.

These white guys were married to white or black women. When color no longer mattered from the laws on the books via amendments, bad residues in old laws were still around and still needed to be fixed. Suffrage was one of them.

Thankfully, black and woman suffrage are now part of the deal. It's been like this for over 100 years so let's get rid of the notion of racism or sexism as precepts of the US government. It has been corrected. Today at worst it is an individual thing.

Just as there are blacks and women who hate whites and men, there surely are whites and men who hate blacks and women. So what? Should we arrest them all? This amendment is one of those necessary to remove the stigmas of sex and racism in the voting process. America was surely trying to get itself right.

XX.

The Twentieth Amendment was adopted primarily for the purpose of abolishing "lame duck" sessions of Congress. It changes the dates when the terms of the President, senators and representatives shall begin and end. The presidential term now begins on January 20 every fourth year, and the terms of senators and representatives begin on January 3, the length of term remaining six and two years, respectively. Consequently a new Congress convenes in the January following the presidential election of the preceding November.

Since only 17 days elapse between the convening of Congress on January 3 and the inauguration of the President on January 20, it is possible that embarrassment may arise in case of delay in counting and declaring the electoral vote, or in electing a President by the House in the event of failure of the electors to elect. The amendment provides that if the President-elect shall have died before inauguration day the Vice President-elect shall be President; and that if a President shall not have been chosen or shall have failed to qualify by inauguration day, the Vice President-elect shall act as President until a President shall have qualified. Congress is authorized to provide for filling a vacancy occurring through failure of both a President-elect and Vice President-elect to qualify, and the person selected shall act until a President or Vice President shall have qualified.

Congress has provided that it shall meet in joint session on January 6 following a presidential election, to count the electoral vote and declare the result. This allows only three days for organization of the House of Representatives by the election of a Speaker. Serious difficulties might arise if the House should fail to organize in time to count the vote, or to elect a President if that duty should fall upon it. Failure of the House to elect a President might be attended by failure of the Senate to elect a Vice President. It is quite conceivable, also, that passions might be aroused if failure to elect a President by a House controlled by one political party should be followed by election of a Vice President by a Senate controlled by another party. It is also conceivable that the two houses of Congress might deadlock upon the selection of a person to fill a vacancy in the Presidency.

XXI.

The Twenty-first Amendment repeals the Eighteenth Amendment and prohibits the transportation or importation into any State of intoxicating liquors in violation of its laws.

XXII

The 22nd amendment limits the president to only two 4 year terms in office. Before the 22nd amendment, Presidents traditionally served two terms, following the example of George Washington. Franklin D Roosevelt broke this tradition during his presidency and served four terms, as World War II and the Great Depression convinced him to run for a third and fourth term, since the country was in crisis. After FDR died in 1945, many Americans began to recognize that having a president serve more than eight years was bad for the country. This led to the 22nd amendment, which was passed by Congress in 1947 and ratified by the states by 1951

XXIII

The 23rd Amendment to the US Constitution was passed by Congress on March 29, 1961. It provides the District of Columbia with the ability to vote for president and vice-president. Up until this time, individuals who lived in the District of Columbia were unable to vote for the president since they did not live in a state and presidential electors were determined based on the number of representatives and senators a state had. This set the number of electors for the District of Columbia equal to that of the least populous state which means that it has three electors.

XXIV

The 24th amendment was important to the Civil Rights Movement as it ended mandatory poll taxes that prevented many African Americans from voting. The rationale for the amendment was that poll taxes, combined with grandfather clauses and intimidation, effectively prevented African Americans from having any sort of political power, especially in the South. When the 24th amendment passed, five southern states, Virginia, Alabama, Texas, Arkansas, and Mississippi still had poll taxes. Most Southern states, at one time or another had poll taxes and in severe cases, had cumulative poll taxes that required the voter to pay taxes not just from that year, but also previous years they had not voted.

Admittedly poll taxes are inherently unfair but Americans being lied to by government is also unfair, and unfortunately, there are American parties that try to trick the least capable of US to discern the message that they will lose their ability to live if X is not elected over Y, even if X is a rapist, a murderer, or a simple political cheat—a thief so to speak.

All men are created equal for sure, and poll taxes may not be proper but permitting the simple minded among us to vote for such important notions is also not fair as they are affected by the messages of the tricksters.

Today, we should have a means of telling a lie from the truth, and any politician who lies should be disqualified from the opportunity of office. If it is discerned by judges that such messages would cause those who would otherwise not know better that they had been lied to then, and I do not know how to do this, their votes would not count. We the People want an informed electorate to vote for important offices. We should figure out how to eliminate those who have no clue who is running from being the deciding votes. .

That is the truth. Unfortunately, our laws do not force politicians to tell the truth or go to jail. Either we have huge prison penalties for lying officials in office and in their candidacies or we need poll gimmicks to prevent the easily influenced by lies to not influence important elections. You tell me how we do that? Otherwise, the least capable people in America will choose who runs our country!

XXV

If the President of the United State dies in office, the Vice President will assume the position of the presidency. Although this is the law today, this was not always the case prior to the 25th amendment. In fact, it was never actually clear in the Constitution that the Vice-President takes over for the President. The Vice-President has taken over for the President several times in our history, usually after the president has been killed or dies of sickness and the first time this happened was when John Tyler, the 10th president, became president after William Henry Harrison died after a month as President. The 25th amendment allows for the Vice President to become president in the event of death, resignation, removal from office or impairment that prevents the current president from fulfilling his or her duties.

The Vice-presidency had been clearly defined by the 12th amendment as the running mate of the sitting president. As such, there is no risk that a member of the opposing party will gain the presidency in the event of the president being unable to serve his or her duties. Among the more important provisions of the 25th amendment are the provisions for the "Acting President." During this condition, the Vice-President temporarily assumes the role of the President as it is assumed that the President is unable to fulfill his or her duties at the moment but will be able to in the very near future.

The 25th amendment was adopted by the states in 1967 with Nebraska and Wisconsin being the first states to ratify it and Nevada the 38th and last state needed to have a ¾ majority

XXVI

The 26th Amendment to the US Constitution was passed by Congress on March 23, 1971 and ratified on July 1, 1971, all during the Vietnam War. The amendment provided the right to vote to individuals who were eighteen years of age. Previous to this, the 14th Amendment had set the voting age at 21. Very strong feelings existed that if people were old enough to serve and die for their country, they should also be able to vote for those people sending them to war.

XXVII

The 27th Amendment to the US Constitution prohibits any law that increases or decreases the salary of members of Congress from taking effect until the start of the next set of terms of office for Representatives. It is the most recent amendment to the United States Constitution. It was submitted by Congress to the states for ratification on September 25, 1789, and became part of the United States Constitution in May 1992, a record-setting period of 202 years, 7 months and 12 days. As we examine rights in this book, the politicians of yesteryear submitted this item to be in the original bill of rights as the second amendment. It was rejected then and somewhat recently has passed and thus its new sequence is amendment # 27.

Conclusion

I decided that the conclusion for this chapter should mostly be written by Sol Bloom. It is from his 150th Anniversary Book re-mastered by Lets Go Publish! And titled, Sol Bloom's ... Epoch Story of the Constitution.

From the time I read his book I have been impressed with the late Congressman Bloom. He is in my opinion a 1937 version of America's founders. I have used many of his thoughts in the chapters we have already discussed. I give you many of his original thoughts in the conclusion below, though I have altered some of the notions as written to fit the times. To get the original, feel free to read Bloom's book.

www.bookhawkers.com

Here is the Chapter Conclusion, which not so coincidentally is also the conclusion of Sol Bloom's Book on the Constitution.

"As the symmetry of arrangement and beautiful co-ordination of motion in the several governments constituting the American system may be compared with the solar system.

"As the Sun is the center of attraction and controlling power that binds and moves the planets in one system, so the People are the center and controlling power that binds and moves their governments in one system.

"The Law which the solar system obeys is not written, but its operation is partly disclosed and partly understood. The Law which the American political system obeys is partly written, for all men to read. It is the Constitution of the United States.

"The limits of the powers of the Sun and the People are not known. They have never been tested to the limit. The composition of the Sun is hidden in Nature. The composition of the People is hidden in human nature.

"Reason assumes that the Sun has powers beyond those known to us. Reason reinforced by knowledge asserts that the People have reserved powers which never have been expressed in written law.

"The United States and the States may be compared to planets revolving around their Sun, the People.

"In order to comprehend the peculiar nature of the American system it must be borne in mind that the States existed before the United States was created. It was to bind them together, to swing them into their coordinated orbits that the Union was perfected.

"Some of the powers possessed by the People are exerted in the States. Others are kept in reserve.

"The powers necessary to bind the States together in one solar Union are set forth in the Constitution. All other powers are kept in reserve.

"The States perform certain functions which the United States cannot perform. The United States performs functions which the States separately cannot perform. The People retain a sphere of personal liberties into which neither the States nor the United States can enter.

"The law which controls the solar system is divine, and therefore perfect. The law which controls the American political system is human, and therefore imperfect. But under a trial of 150 years [when Bloom wrote his book in 1937], it has been found to approach more nearly the symmetry of the law that rules the universe than any other emanation of the human mind and will.

"Several unique features of the Constitution distinguish it from any previous inventions in the art of government. Among these are: The Constitution binds individuals as well as States. Under it all individuals have equal duties and rights.

"The legislative, executive, and judicial powers are lodged in separate bodies of public servants whose powers and duties compel them to check and balance one another. No uncontrolled power is lodged in any one. The written Constitution is made paramount to any legislative, executive, or judicial authority.

"A court is created with power to hold all authorities within their allotted spheres, and this court itself is bound to remain within its allotted sphere. The Constitution contains within itself a method whereby it may be amended by the People.

"These principles, never practiced before, are the bone and sinew of a fabric suitable to a nation whose government obeys those whom it rules, and whose people rule the government which they obey."

End of Sol Bloom's Conclusion.

I surely wish I could write as well as Sol Bloom to help us all understand why being an American, born of the Founders and of Sol Bloom's sweat labor, is such a big deal. We Americans are all so lucky!

Chapter 16 Constitutional Rights, Powers and Duties

The people or the government?

The Bill of Rights is the collective name for the first ten amendments to the United States Constitution. It helps to repeat that often when one is learning the concepts of our founding government. As you may know from earlier reading in this book, the Bill if Rights was proposed to quiet the fears of Anti-Federalists who had opposed Constitutional ratification.

The ten (originally twelve) amendments were brought forth to guarantee a number of personal freedoms (rights), limit the government's power in judicial and other proceedings, and reserve some powers to the states and the public.

Originally the amendments applied only to the federal government. However, most were subsequently applied to the government of each state by way of the Fourteenth Amendment to the Constitution, through a process known as incorporation.

Let's recap how these rights were introduced to Congress. On June 8, 1789 Representative James Madison introduced a series of thirty-nine amendments (Lots more than the twelve which were approved) to the constitution in the House of Representatives. Among his recommendations Madison proposed opening up the Constitution and inserting specific rights directly into the articles of the Constitution. His notions limited the power of Congress beginning in Article

One, Section 9. At the time the founders figured Congress had the real power and there would be no need to limit the power of the chief executive as Congress could theoretically do that by itself.

Seven of these limitations would eventually become part of the ten ratified Bill of Rights as amendments. Ultimately, on September 25, 1789, Congress approved twelve articles of amendment to the Constitution and submitted them to the states for ratification. Many of the Anti-Federalists wanted the Constitution itself, within in its main body, not in adjunct form, to delineate the rights of the people of the nation. Madison's original proposal provided for that.

Contrary to Madison's original proposal that the articles be incorporated into the main body of the Constitution, they were eventually proposed as "supplemental" additions to it. On December 15, 1791, Articles Three–Twelve, having been ratified by the required number of states, became renumbered as Amendments One–Ten of the Constitution. These ten ratified amendments were the Bill of Rights as passed and became a part of the Constitution forever.

On May 7, 1992, after an unprecedented period of 202 years, 225 days, the original submitted and not ratified Amendment # 2, known then as Article Two crossed the Constitutional threshold for ratification and became the Twenty-seventh Amendment and the last amendment as of 2014. As a result, the original Article One (the original 1st amendment) alone remains unratified and still pending before the states.

The Bill of Rights enumerates freedoms not explicitly indicated in the main body of the Constitution, such as freedom of religion, freedom of speech, a free press, and free assembly; the right to keep and bear arms; freedom from unreasonable search and seizure, security in personal effects, and freedom from warrants issued without probable cause; indictment by a grand jury for any capital or "infamous crime"; guarantee of a speedy, public trial with an impartial jury; and prohibition of double jeopardy.

In addition, the Bill of Rights reserves for the people any rights not specifically mentioned in the Constitution and reserves all powers not specifically granted to the federal government for the people or the States. The Bill was influenced by George Mason's 1776 Virginia Declaration of Rights, the English Bill of Rights 1689, and earlier English political documents such as Magna Charta (1215 A.D.).

The Bill of Rights had little judicial impact for the first 150 years of its existence, but was the basis for many Supreme Court decisions of the 20th and 21st centuries. One of the first fourteen copies of the Bill of Rights is on public display at the National Archives in Washington, D.C.

What rights / powers do we the people have and what rights / powers do we the people not have? What rights / powers does the government have and which ones does it not have? All Americans should want to know the answers to those questions. And so we have a ton of rights and powers to discuss in the rest of this chapter. Since this is a book about the Bill of Rights it is a good idea to define a right as well as a power or a duty so that we get a clear picture of what the Constitution and the Bill of Rights delivers to us

What is a right? A right is a moral or legal entitlement to have or obtain something or to act in a certain way

What is a power? A power is the ability to do something or act in a particular way, especially as a faculty or quality. Also, a power can be defined as the possession of control or command over others; authority.

What is a duty? A duty is a moral or legal obligation; a responsibility. It can also be a task or action that someone is required to perform.

The following outline describes in brief the more important rights, powers, and duties recognized or established in the U.S. Constitution, in Common Law as it existed at the time the U.S. Constitution was adopted, or as implied therein.

Not included in this outline are certain "internal" or administrative rights and powers that pertain to the various elements of government within each level with respect to each other. This chapter is just big enough to give us a proper perspective on what the Constitution along with the Bill of Rights provide for all Americans.

Most of the content in this outline is supplied by the Constitution Society. We have changed some text for brevity, clarification, and/or style changes. We give our thanks to The Constitution Society for their great work: www.constitution.org

Let's continue our definitions below to set the stage for the discussion or rights, powers, and duties. Let's first examine the notion of "personhood," and then go from there.

Personhood: "Persons" are one of the two main classes which are the subject of rights, powers, and duties, the other being "citizens". Persons may be "natural" or "corporate". Yes, according to the Supreme Court of the United States (SCOTUS), corporations are to be treated as legal citizens.

"Citizens" are a subclass of "natural persons". Only persons have standing as parties under due process. Each government has the power to define what is and is not a "person" within its jurisdiction, subject to certain restrictions of Common Law and the Constitution, the 15th Amendment to which requires that it not exclude anyone based on race, color, or previous condition of servitude.

Under Common Law existing at the time of the adoption of the U.S. Constitution, "natural personhood" was considered to begin at natural birth and end with the cessation of the heartbeat. But technology has created a new situation, opening the way for statute or court decision to extend this definition and set the conditions under which personhood begins and ends.

Each government may also establish, within its jurisdiction, "corporate persons" such as governmental entities, associations, trusts, corporations, or partnerships, in addition to the Common Law "natural" persons, but the "personhood" of such corporate entities is not created by the government. Its corporate personhood derives from the personhood of its members. Corporate persons must be aggregates of natural persons.

Citizenship: Citizenship is the attribute of persons who, as members of the polity, have certain privileges and duties in addition to those they have as persons. Citizens include those born on U.S. or State territory or naturalized according to law.

Natural Rights: The classic definition of "natural rights" are "life, liberty, and property", but these need to be expanded somewhat. They are rights of "personhood", not "citizenship". These rights are not all equally basic, but form a hierarchy of derivation, with those listed later being generally derived from those listed earlier.

What is Personal Security (Life)?
(1) Not to be killed.
(2) Not to be injured or abused.

What is Personal Liberty?
(3) To move freely.
(4) To assemble peaceably.
(5) To keep and bear arms
(6) To assemble in an independent well-disciplined[13] militia.
(7) To communicate with the world.
(8) To express or publish one's opinions or those of others.
(9) To practice one's religion.
(10) To be secure in one's person, house, papers, vehicle[14], and effects against unreasonable searches and seizures.
(11) To enjoy privacy in all matters in which the rights of others are not violated.[7]
What is Private Property?
(12) To acquire, have and use the means necessary to exercise the above natural rights and pursue happiness, specifically including:
  — A private residence, from which others may be excluded.
  — Tools needed for one's livelihood.
  — Personal property, which others may be denied the use of.
  — Arms suitable for personal and community defense.

What are non-natural rights of personhood,created by social contract?

(1) To enter into contracts, and thereby acquire contractual rights, to secure the means to exercise the above natural rights.[1,15]
(2) To enjoy equally the rights, privileges and protections of personhood as established by law.
(3) To petition an official for redress of grievances and get action thereon in accordance with law, subject to the resources available thereto.
(4) To petition a legislator and get consideration thereof, subject to resources available thereto.
(5) To petition a court for redress of grievances and get a decision thereon, subject to resources available thereto.
(6) Not to have one's natural rights individually disabled except through due process of law, which includes:

(A) IN CRIMINAL PROSECUTIONS:
1. Not to be charged for a major crime but by indictment by a Grand Jury, except while serving in the military, or while serving in the Militia during time of war or public danger.
2. Not to be charged more than once for the same offense.
3. Not to be compelled to testify against oneself.
4. Not to have excessive bail required.
5. To be tried by an impartial jury from the state and district in which the events took place.
6. To have a jury of at least six for a misdemeanor, and at least twelve for a felony.[1]
7. To a speedy trial.
8. To a public trial.
9. To have the assistance of counsel of one's choice.
10. To be informed of the nature and cause of the accusation.
11. To be confronted with the witnesses against one.
12. To have compulsory process for obtaining favorable witnesses.
13. To have each charge proved beyond a reasonable doubt.[1]
14. To have a verdict by a unanimous vote of the jury, which shall not be held to account for its verdict.[1]
15. To have the jury decide on both the facts of the case and the constitutionality, jurisdiction, and applicability of the law.[1]
16. Upon conviction, to have each disablement separately and explicitly proven as justified and necessary based on the facts and verdict.[1]
17. To have a sentence which explicitly states all disablements, and is final in that once rendered no further disablements may be imposed for the same offense.[1]

18. Not to have a cruel or unusual punishment inflicted upon oneself.

(B) IN CIVIL CASES:
1. To trial by an impartial jury from the state and district in which the events took place[1] where the issue in question is either a natural right[1] or property worth more than $20.
2. In taking of one's property for public use, to be given just compensation therefor.
3. To have compulsory process for obtaining favorable witnesses.

(C) IN ALL CASES:
1. To have process only upon legal persons able to defend themselves, either natural persons or corporate persons that are represented by a natural person as agent, and who are present, competent, and duly notified, except, in cases of disappearance or abandonment, after public notice and a reasonable period of time
2. Not to be ordered to give testimony or produce evidence beyond what is necessary to the proper conduct of the process

What are Non-natural rights or citizenship, created by social contract?
(1) To enjoy equally the rights and privileges of citizenship as established by law.
(2) To vote in elections that are conducted fairly and honestly, by secret ballot.
(3) To exercise general police powers to defend the community and enforce the laws, subject to legal orders of higher-ranking officials
(4) To receive militia training.
See also List of constitutional rights.

Disabilities of minority: Certain of the above rights are restricted, or "disabled", for minors, but the definition of who is a minor and the extent to which each of these rights are disabled for minors, is limited to the jurisdiction over which each government has general legislative authority, which for the U.S. government, is "federal ground" (see below). Minors are the only class of persons whose rights may be disabled without a need to justify the disablement as arising from the need to resolve a conflict with the rights of others, either through statute or due process. The disablement consists of the assignment of a power to supervise the exercise of the rights under the headings of "liberty" and "property" listed above to a guardian, by default the parents, who acts as agent of the State for the purpose of nurturing the minor. The disability is normally removed by statute providing for removal when a certain age, such as 18, or condition, such as marriage, is attained. The disabilities of minority can also be removed earlier by court order or, if statute allows, extended beyond the usual statutory expiration by court order in cases of incompetence. The right to vote is not included among the disabilities of minority, but is defined separately by law, so that removal of the disabilities of minority does not in itself affect having the right to vote.

What are Constitutional duties of persons under U.S. or State jurisdiction?
(1) To obey laws that are constitutional and applied within their proper jurisdiction and according to their intent.
(2) To comply with the terms of legal contracts to which one is a party.
(3) To tell the truth under oath.

What are Constitutional duties of citizens under U.S. or State jurisdiction?
(1) To preserve, protect, and defend the Constitution.[6]
(2) To help enforce laws and practices that are constitutional and applied within their proper jurisdiction and according to their intent, and to resist those which are not.
(3) To serve on juries, and to render verdicts according to the constitutionality, jurisdiction, and applicability of statute and common law, and the facts of the case.

What are Constitutional duties of able-bodied citizens under U.S. or State jurisdiction?
(1) To defend the U.S. or State, individually and through service in the Militia.
(2) To keep and bear arms.[18]
(3) To exercise general police powers to defend the community and enforce the laws, subject to legal orders of higher-ranking officials when present.[17]

What are the Powers delegated to U.S. (National) Governmen?
A. EXCLUSIVE POWERS
(1) To lay and collect import duties.[8]
(2) To pay the debts of the U.S. Government.
(3) To regulate commerce with foreign nations and Indian Tribes.
(4) To regulate commerce among the States.[2]
(5) To regulate immigration.[7]
(6) To establish a uniform rule of naturalization.

(7) To establish uniform laws on bankruptcy throughout the United States.

(8) To coin money and regulate its value and that of foreign coin, and to issue bills of credit.

(9) To provide for the punishment of counterfeiting the securities and current coin of the United States.[3]

(10) To fix the standard of weights and measures.

(11) To provide and regulate postal services.

(12) To establish protection for intellectual property, including patent, copyright, and trademark rights.

(13) To constitute lower national courts.

(14) To define and punish piracies and felonies committed on the high seas, and offenses against the laws of nations.[3]

(15) To declare war, authorize warlike activities by other than the armed forces, and make rules concerning captures.

(16) To raise, support and regulate the armed forces.

(17) To govern what part of the Militia shall be employed in the service of the United States.

(18) To exercise general Legislation[9] over federal ground, which is limited to federal territories and districts, land purchased from states with the consent of their legislatures, U.S. flag vessels on the high seas, and the grounds of U.S. embassies abroad.

(19) To guarantee a republican form[12] of government to the States.[3]

(20) To enter into a treaty, alliance, or confederation with a foreign state.

(21) To declare the punishment for treason.[3]

(22) To prescribe the manner in which the acts, records, and judicial proceedings of each state shall be proved to other states and what should be done about them.

(23) To admit new states into the Union.

(24) To dispose of and make all needful Rules and Regulations respecting the Territory or other Property belonging to the United States.

(25) To make laws necessary and proper for executing the powers delegated to the U.S. government.

B. PRE-EMPTIVE BUT NON-EXCLUSIVE POWERS

(1) To provide for the common defense and general welfare.

(2) To provide for calling forth the Militia to execute the laws, suppress insurrections, and repel invasions.[16]

(3) To provide for organizing, arming, and disciplining the Militia.

(4) To prescribe the times, places and manner of holding elections for members of Congress, except the places for electing senators.

(5) To conduct a census every ten years.

C. NON-PRE-EMPTIVE NON-EXCLUSIVE POWERS
(1) To lay and collect excise taxes on commerce or income taxes on persons.[8]
(2) To borrow money.

What are the Restrictions of the powers of the national Government:
(1) No exercise of powers not delegated to it by the Constitution.
(2) No payment from the Treasury except under appropriations made by law.
(3) Excises and duties must be uniform throughout the United States.
(4) Shall pass no tax or duty on articles exported from any state.[5]
(5) No appointment of a senator or representative to any civil office which was created while he was a member of Congress or for which the amount of compensation was increased during that period.
(6) No preferences to the ports of one state over another in regulation or tax collection.
(7) No titles of nobility shall be granted by the U.S. government, or permitted to be granted to government officials by foreign states.
(8) May not protect a State against domestic violence without the request of its legislature, unless it cannot be convened, in which case, without the consent of its executive.
(9) U.S. courts do not have jurisdiction over suits against a state by citizens of another state or foreign country.

What are Powers delegated to State Governments?
A. EXCLUSIVE POWERS
(1) To appoint persons to fill vacancies in the U.S. Congress from that state and to hold special elections to replace them. State executive may make temporary appointments if state legislature in recess and until they reconvene, when they shall appoint a temporary replacement.
(2) To appoint the officers of its Militia.
(3) To conduct the training of its Militia.

B. NON-EXCLUSIVE POWERS
(1) To prescribe the times, places and manner of holding elections for members of Congress.

What are restrictions of the powers of the State Governments?
(1) State constitutions and laws may not conflict with any provision of the U.S. Constitution or U.S. laws pursuant to it.
(2) May not exercise powers not delegated to the State government by the State Constitution.

(3) May not make anything but gold or silver coin a tender in payment of debts.
(4) May not pass a law impairing the obligation of contracts.
(5) May not grant a title of nobility.
(6) May not collect imposts or duties on imports or exports without consent of Congress, except fees necessary to cover the costs of inspections and paid to the U.S. Treasury.
(7) May not lay a duty on tonnage.
(8) May not keep troops or ships of war in time of peace or make war without the consent of Congress, unless actually invaded and in imminent danger that does not admit of delay.
(9) May not make a compact or agreement with another state of the U.S. or with a foreign state without the consent of Congress.

What are duties of the State Governments?
(1) Must provide a republican form of government to their citizens.
(2) Must conduct honest and fair elections, by secret ballot.
(3) Must give full faith and credit to the public acts, records, and judicial proceedings of every other state, and recognize the privileges and immunities granted thereby.
(4) Must extradite a person charged with a crime in another state to that state.
(5) Must organize and train their militias.

What are restrictions of the powers of all Governments:
(1) Shall not disable any natural or constitutional right without due process of law, and then only to the extent necessary to avoid infringing the rights of others.
(2) Shall not deny any person within its jurisdiction equal protection of the laws.
(3) Shall not suspend habeas corpus, except in case of rebellion of invasion and the public safety may require it.
(4) Shall not issue a search warrant but on probably cause, supported by an oath or affirmation, and particularly describing the place to be searched, and the person or things to be seized.
(5) Shall not arrest members of Congress, except for treason, felony, or breach of the peace, while their house is in session.
(6) Shall not question a member of Congress on anything he says during a speech or debate in his house.
(7) Shall not pass any bill of attainder or ex post facto law.
(8) Shall allow no slavery or involuntary servitude except as punishment for a crime of which the party shall have been duly convicted.
(9) Shall not deny or abridge the right to vote to any person on account of race, color, previous condition of servitude, sex, for failure to pay any tax, or on account of age if older than 18.

(10) Shall not exercise any power in an unreasonable manner or for other than a legitimate public purpose, as partially indicated in the Preamble. (No power is "plenary", and discretion can be abused.)

What are some arguably needed national powers?
(1) To regulate the manufacture, distribution, operation, and disposition of aircraft and spacecraft, the regulation of their crews, and the definition and punishment of crimes committed on U.S. registered aircraft or spacecraft or on aircraft or spacecraft operating in U.S. airspace.
(2) To regulate cabled or wireless communications beyond a distance of 1 kilometer.
(3) To regulate the production, distribution, and use of nuclear energy, and electric energy transmitted more than 1 kilometer.
(4) To limit tort liability on commerce and commercial articles subject to U.S. regulation of their manufacture.
(5) To pre-emptively pass and enforce laws needed to conserve wildlife and natural resources, to protect the climate and natural environment, to prevent an excess of population, and to regulate public health and workplace safety.
(6) To provide for the punishment of abuses of power by any official, agent, or employee of, or contractor for, any institution of government, and specifically any violations of the Constitution and laws pursuant thereto.
(7) To provide for the punishment of abuses of the natural rights of persons by other persons, in the event that those abuses, if the occurred on state ground, are not prosecuted by a State government.
(8) To define "due process" to include the elements given above which are not now explicit in the U.S. Constitution.
(9) To define the arms to which persons have a right to keep and bear as including "all those weapons which may be carried by one person and which might be useful or necessary to defend oneself or the community, except weapons of mass destruction such as bombs, heavy missiles or artillery, or biological, chemical, or nuclear agents which may cause lasting injury or death."
(10) To make explicit that only natural persons or corporate persons composed of natural persons may be the subject of due process in any civil or criminal proceeding.

NOTES: Feel free to go to www.constitution.org/powright.htm to see their whole section on rights. In this, they show a series of notes associated with the delineated rights, powers, and duties shown above.

FURTHER COMMENT by the Constitution Society—very interesting:

Note that there is no right to marry or bear children included among any of the rights listed above. It is not a "natural" right, because natural rights are only rights of individuals, and exercise of a "right" to marry, without the consent of the other, would be an assault.

Since consent is required, it is a matter of contract, and contractual rights are created by the community, even if it is a "community" of only two persons. Since the community is normally a larger polity, and since all legal contracts are agreements not only between the contracting parties, but also with the entire community, therefore the community has the power to regulate marriage and childbirth, and has exercised that power since time immemorial, for the benefit of the community.

Note also that the fundamental unit of the social contract is the local community, ward, or village. These may aggregate into a larger "state" or "federal union", but the basis is agreement among those who are in direct contact with one another.

It is sometimes thought that "the Constitution" consists only of the written document. This is not so. The title "The Constitution of the United States" was added after the document was adopted, but "constitution" meant the "basic legal order", and the Constitution consists of both the written document and the common law at the time the document was adopted, which is here referred to as the Common Law in caps. Now, the written document does supersede the Common Law where they might be in conflict, but it does not replace it, and courts must refer to the Common Law for guidance where the written document is silent or ambiguous.

In addition to the written document and the Common Law, the Constitution also includes Treaties, which, although they are valid only insofar as they are not in conflict with the written Constitution, are superior to both the Common Law and to State constitutions and laws, to the extent that those might be in conflict with the Treaties. Thus, some of the Treaties that have been adopted extend and clarify some of the rights, powers, and duties provided in the written Constitution. For example, that is how "federal ground" is extended to include coastal waters out to a certain distance from shore, and the grounds of U.S. embassies abroad, and how the rights of the people are amplified by the Charter of the United Nations and by various bilateral and multilateral Treaties that extend civil and commercial rights to U.S. citizens abroad.

On its website, www.constitution.org/powright.htm, the Constitution society provides a number of clarifying diagrams to help clarify the relationship among the various elements of law in the U.S. legal system.

Each element is superior to the one below it, although state constitutions are derived from their people, not from the U.S. Constitution. Although not shown, each element also includes the body of writings and recorded speeches of the legislators, diplomats, and judges who wrote the constitutions, treaties, laws, and court decisions, which clarify their intent, and which must be accepted as the basis of interpreting the words as originally meant and understood when there is confusion or dispute over their meaning.

Nested
constitutions

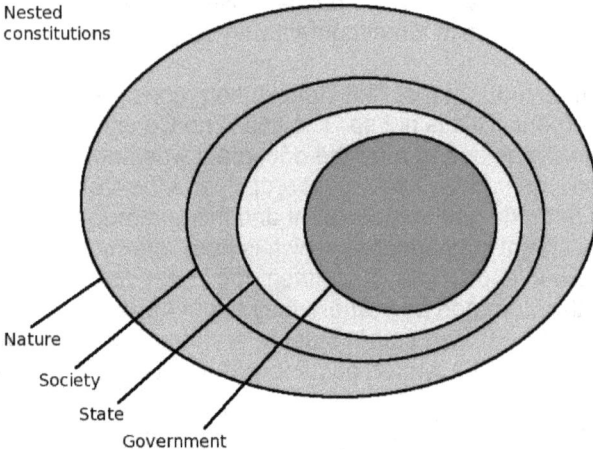

Nature

Society

State

Government

Public Action

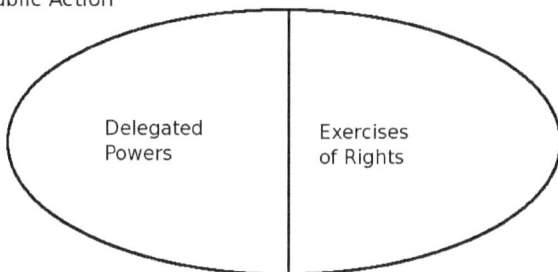

Each delegation of a power restricts rights.
Each declaration of a right restricts delegated powers.

A right (immunity) may be expressed as a restriction
on a power, and a power as a restriction on a right.

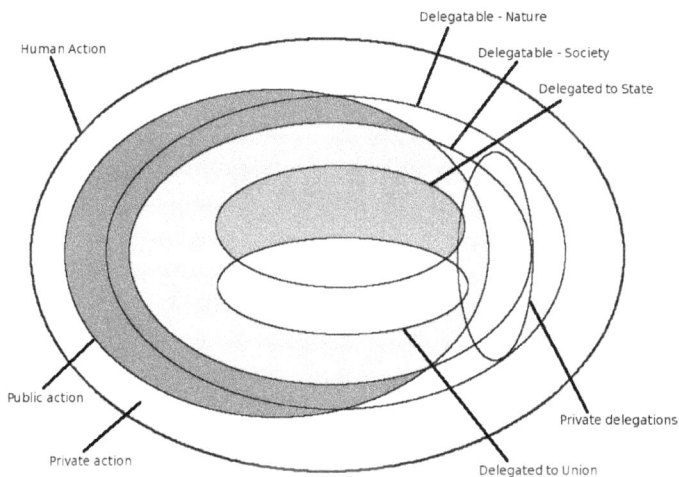

Chapter 17   The Bill of Rights Made the Constitution OK for All!

The fight over the Bill of Rights

Now, that you and I have exhaustingly traversed multiple chapters, in search of the perfect founding of our nation along with a "perfect" Bill of Rights, should we believe that we have found it? I say yes!

The Constitution of the United States of America contains the Bill of Rights. Not only does it contain the whole Bill of Rights but it is based on a long line of other historical documents that add even more meaning to the Constitution and American rights as we find ourselves at times trying to understand exactly what the Founders meant here and there. And, thus it has been quite proper to discuss most of these documents before we move to the real purpose of this book, The US Bill of Rights.

The "perfect Bill of Rights," is thus based on the "perfect Constitution." In its own rules, the Constitution prescribes a way for it to be changed, as long as the people agree. Who can ask for anything more?

In order for the Constitution to have been ratified and to become the operating supreme law of the Land, the USA, the Founders convinced detractors that they would use the rules in the Constitution itself to change it to suit the detractor's needs. The Bill of Rights in fact, was the first set of changes to the US Constitution, and it satisfied the objections of the original detractors or the Constitution would exist only in the history books and not as the law of the land.

The Constitution offers no opportunity for the congress or the president to choose to act other than directed by the articles within this document as well as the laws enacted by the Congress. In terms of the forty-fourth President, we know that there are a number of accusations of lawlessness. See Chapter 17. Nobody other than the people can change the Constitution—even the president of the United States, as hard as he may try.

The laws broken by the 2014 current administration include violations of the pure Constitution and a number of other laws that have been enacted by Congress, which the current President, as all presidents has taken an oath to enforce. The current President has no problem with calling a weak Congress's bluff and so he chooses his laws carefully, and thus, he reigns, un-impeached.

However, more and more citizens are finding the lawlessness of the Executive Branch a little too much to stomach, in the America they understand, and they are demanding Congress act to assure that the Constitution in totality is upheld and not disregarded as trivial. Check out Chapter 17 for a more perfect view of the *Constitutional Problems of 2014*.

The Constitution, though a phenomenally "more perfect" instrument of government for America than the Articles of Confederation, is still not 100% perfect. Nothing is perfect! As I like to say in its defense, it is more perfect than any other supreme body of law in any other country, including Bimini, which is a beautiful island in the Bahamas—where I think I would rather be than right here, right now!

If this were not so, I too would definitely be seeking refuge in Bimini, or the next most free country in the world. Right now, because of our Constitution, and the expressed Bill of Rights, we would find the only country that provides full freedom and liberty in all cases to be the United States of America. Though some politicians may have bought the stamp, there is no expiration date on the United States.

Americans paying attention know that the best set of laws for both the hoi polloi (regular people) and the hoity-toity (the elite among us) is our one of a kind US Constitution.

The Bill of Rights is essential in that it spells out in bold detail, the fundamental rights of all Americans including the rights of free assembly, free speech, freedom to practice religion, and many other rights including the right to bear arms. Some Presidents of recent time would like to do away with these rights.

Many ask why, with such a fine Constitution is a separate *"Bill of Rights"* required? If the Constitution is almost perfect, why was it not enough? Why is it not enough? "Why did we ever need a *Bill of Rights*? We have broached this subject in past chapters but let's take it head on again.

In this modern era, where all traditional values are questioned, there is a film and a video game known as the *Bill of Rights*. Perhaps you know of this. Perhaps you have seen it or heard about it. Both media notions (film & video game) attempt to tell the story about a struggle among the Founders and the Framers of the US Constitution that nearly tore the nation apart. We have discussed this but let's go again.

It was even before the US had a Constitution to assure its future. Toward the end of the 16 minute documentary, the *Bill of Rights* is described as "absolutely essential to our national character."

When the Founders were founding the nation, there was no notion of political parties, and that is why the brave men of those times were able to come together to delineate a set of laws that would be able to guide America forever. There were

no Republicans and there were no Democrats. Everybody
was for America.

Even then, of course there was the risk of a scoundrel in an
important office, who might be un-American, and that
scoundrel, even if he were the President, might choose to
ignore the laws of the country, passed or not passed in his or
her administration.

Therefore, the folks at that time, some who believed the
Constitution was perfect, and others who thought that our
rights needed to be declared outwardly in a positive sense,
needed to come together.

The Constitution gave the people all the power but to be fair,
the specific rights were not delineated. And, so an errant
judge in the future, wrong as he or she might be, could decree
that there is no right in the Constitution guaranteeing you
freedom of speech or assembly. The judge would be wrong
but, then what happens when you find yourself in prison?

The Bill of Rights therefore specifically, forcefully, and more
authoritatively defines the fundamental rights of the
American people. Some people in 1787 had a major issue
about whether the US Constitution restricted government
powers sufficiently enough to assure that Americans had
perpetual liberty under the law. Today's citizens can
understand why!

If Government had no power to restrict the power of the
people, then why should the people need a specific bill of
rights? The simple answer is that after hundreds of years of
tyranny in their home countries, the colonists trusted nobody,
and they therefore recognized the possibility of an errant
judge or powerful government of the future misunderstanding
the Constitution, and going it alone without the Congress or
the people.

The framers of The Constitution gave no implicit rights to government other than those so enumerated specifically in the Constitution. There were few of these as enumerated in Chapter 15. So, many of the framers did not believe that the people needed a bill of rights since government could theoretically never take away the inalienable rights the people already possessed.

The Constitution gave the government no power to override the will of the people. Others were concerned that since people are people, scoundrels might emerge as leaders and the people would have no backup column to present to prove their rights. And, so many smart Americans looked for a specific Bill of Rights!

Implication or Specification?

The battle of whether a Bill of Rights was necessary during the founding and framing of the Constitution is a matter of implication or specification. Those who believed the government was sufficiently verboten from taking away individual liberty saw no reason to specify (specification) the liberties that could not be taken away.

Their answer was "no liberties" can be taken from the people since the Constitution in raw form, un-amended, implicitly defers rights not given to the government as rights which the people implicitly possess. Yet, implicit or explicit, when quoted, we all like to have an explicit quote upon which to base our contention.

Well, the explicits and the implicits got their day of discussion and our Founders worked for the good of all to come up with something that would work. Out of their compromise (The Great Compromise) came one of our nation's most central documents and the foundation for some of our most celebrated freedoms. The document produced to represent their thoughts is forever known as the *Bill of Rights.*

Whether it was needed logically or not needed logically, it is the Bill of Rights nonetheless that guaranteed the ratification of The Constitution. It was enough to convince the patriots that the Constitution was to be approved.

Americans wanted written assurances that the rights they fought for as colonists against Britain in the American Revolution would never be taken away. They believed their rights should be protected by a written document. The Bill of Rights plus the Constitution served that purpose.

Without the Bill of Rights, some of the states had refused to ratify the Constitution because in its first cut, a national Bill of Rights was not included. Thus the Bill of Rights was an essential ingredient to having a Constitution pass the states for ratification.

Without the *Bill of Rights* we would have never been able to ratify the Constitution that brought more stability to our nation. The Constitution and the specifics in the *Bill of Rights* and the other seventeen Amendments have helped our country survive during the times of instability, confusion, and partial insanity concerning how to properly organize and run the nation.

The *Bill of Rights* was carved out after the Constitution had been written. And, though it is deemed by many to be an integral "part" of the Constitution, when offered to the people, it was created independently of the Constitution and presented as an add-on, though a very necessary add-on.

The *Bill of Rights* indeed consists of the first ten approved / ratified amendments to the US Constitution. The original framers trusted that we would never turn on the precepts in the Constitution. Those insisting on the need for a Bill of

Rights wanted to assure themselves that we could not even find a minor loophole in the Constitution to limit our rights.

We all know, and quite often in this book, we have demonstrated how the Constitution guarantees every American certain basic rights including: freedom of speech, freedom of religion, the right to assembly, the right to a jury trial, etc. These and many other rights are implicitly protected by our Constitution. But these freedoms, though implicit, were not explicitly stated in the original version of the Constitution. It took the *Bill of Rights* to mention them explicitly.

You may have already read the full Constitution in this book if you paged to Appendix E. You know that nothing was written in the Constitution to implicitly or specifically grant the freedoms in the Bill of Rights to all Americans. In fact, as noted, many of the Framers of the Constitution were dead set against including such a Bill in the document even if provided as amendments. Like the old TV ad once said, the Framers would answer: "It's in there!"

The Framers were very smart people. They knew that when they had written the Constitution, they had implicitly granted all those provisions in the Bill of Rights simply by denying government such rights. In truth, implicit provisions are far more powerful and long-serving than those explicitly provided.

But, honest regular people at that time, and even in this time, looking for truth have a tough time understanding implicit notions. And, so the explicit provisions of the Bill of Rights helped many Americans, who did not profess to be Constitutional scholars to lean towards the ratification of the Constitution with ten important rights of the people were explicitly noted.

Thus, as the debate ensued, the non-trusting were compelled by their very nature to demand as many explicit provisions from the new government as possible. The colonists did not trust any government at the time—even if their favorite neighbor were president.

As we all know, humans have limited attention spans. Worse than that, historical governments have most often gone bad over time. So, why would the regular folks in America back those wanting votes for the Constitution without "proper" guarantees for liberty and freedom over time?

And, so a look back does say that a Bill of Rights needed to be created and added to the Constitution. James Madison, one of the major authors of the Federalist Papers, and a great patriot, who eventually became the fourth President of the United States was enlisted to write many of the precepts in the Bill of Rights. Like Alexander Hamilton, he was a phenomenal writer. He is credited with being the primary author of the Constitution and so he is known by historians as the "Father of the Constitution."

Ironically, Madison, in his personal thoughts, did not think a Bill of Rights was necessary. He took issue, though lightly, with those who felt that the Constitution needed to grant rights. Instead, he felt that the people had all the rights, according to the Constitution and the government had no rights other than those explicitly granted by the people.

Consequently Madison would have been against any Bill of Rights and the document that emerged from the Constitutional Convention in 1787 reflected his full conviction. He believed the Constitution as it was written already spelled out what the Federal Government could do and could not do. He believed that if it wasn't in that document, it wasn't any of the Federal Government's business. No further protection was necessary. I thank the Lord that he changed his mind.

James Madison never met a 20th or 21st Century leftist politician looking for an excuse to break through the limitations on government provided in the Constitution to further the cause of communism. These scoundrels love their rights yet want the rights of others taken away to suit their interests. Some think that the Bill of Rights has only postponed the villains, who sometimes even outwardly shows disdain for the freedoms granted to Americans by the Constitution.

As recently as late May 2014, for example, the current President challenged the notion of Article II of the Constitution regarding two Senators from each state. The President said it is unfair that hugely populated Democratic States such as New York and California get just two Senators when they have lots more people. If you are reading this book in 2067, it would save some research for you to know that the current President, who presides while I am writing this book, is a leftist long before he is an American.

Will this President, with a lack of any deep love for America and the Constitution, try by Executive Order to change the Constitution? Readers in 2014 already know the answer. Chapter 17 gives a glimpse of more to come.

The President has already done this with other laws such as those pertaining to immigration and social issues. This, of course is why his administration is considered lawless. It helps to remember that many colonists were concerned that a strong national government was a threat to individual rights and that the President might attempt to become a king, and that strengthened their demand for more explicit rights. Thankfully no American President so far at least, has ever tried to convince the people he or she should be King or Queen of America. That time may be right around the corner.

Therefore, to most conservative Americans it is better to explicitly state rights than to have a politician motivated by political opportunism take matters into their own hands.

Why is it that the courts, using impartiality and superior judgment today always break decisions on party lines? Why is it that America and Americans are not the primary focus of the legislature and the courts.

Well, this is not the right book, but if I had my way, I would fire the press first. They are so corrupt they stink. Congress is only a whiff away from being as bad. Would it not be wonderful if political party affiliation and agendas were not how the courts or the Senate or the House would decide issues that are substantive to citizens.

The leaders and the people in colonial time had integrity as a real virtue. Their moms and dads helped them gain such virtue. Even those not on your side were good people and good enough to work for compromises that helped all Americans—not just the Democratic Party.

George Mason, a Virginia delegate vigorously disagreed with James Madison on the notion of a Bill of Rights, yet both were honorable in their disagreement. Mason was not so sure that the new government would provide anything better than the rights the British provided, and then took back when it was convenient. Madison knew the inherent logic in the Constitution should work for all Americans.

Despite being wounded in spirit and in the wallet, Americans in the eighteenth century all knew that a long and bloody war to win independence had only recently ended. Though Madison et al believed they had protected Americans in the text of The Constitution, Mason and others wanted to explicitly ensure that the new government could not erase the freedoms the Patriots had fought so hard to secure.

George Mason declared that he would rather "chop off my right hand" than support a Constitution that did not include a Bill of Rights. What a great patriot!

If we are looking for forefathers of things like Articles and Declarations and Constitutions, we might well credit George Mason as the *Father of the Bill of Rights.*

Depending on your level of trust in the positive precepts of the Constitution as originally written, it is reasonable to believe that the more assurances of freedom the better. Those patriots looking for more assurances won and The Bill of Rights was added to the Constitution as the first ten amendments on December 15, 1791.

The fact that the Constitution did not include a Bill of Rights to specifically protect Americans' hard-won rights had certainly sparked the most heated debates during the ratification process. Now that we know there is such a Bill; what rights do they give?

Let's go over a few for a second or third time as all of us have a tendency to forget important things until we realize how important they really are.

As previously noted, the Bill of Rights are the first ten amendments (changes) to the United States Constitution. Madison saw no real problem with the Bill of Rights other than their redundancy for he already believed they existed implicitly within the Constitution.

Rather than risk destroying the Constitution, Jefferson, out of town during the debate about the Bill of Rights, wrote to Madison advocating their inclusion: "Half a loaf is better than no bread. If we cannot secure all our rights, let us secure what we can." So, Madison introduced the Bill of Rights as a series of amendments on June 8, 1789 in the First Federal Congress.

Who wrote the Bill of Rights? George Mason, who would not sign the Constitution without the Bill of Rights and James Madison, who felt they were not needed, are considered by historians to be among the two primary authors of the twelve articles in the original Bill of Rights.

Ten of the amendments of the twelve were ratified without much debate and they became the Bill of Rights in 1791. These amendments specify rights of citizens explicitly by their content and implicitly by "further" limiting the powers of the federal government. They protect the rights of all citizens, residents and visitors on United States territory. More people today understand the Bill of Rights than those that understand the full impact of the US Constitution.

About the Bill of Rights?

So, what is meant by the term Bill of Rights? It represents the full notion of the first ten amendments to the United States Constitution. Amendments are supposed to be changes even though Madison believed these ten Amendments, and the rights they gave American citizens existed implicitly in the original drafting of the US Constitution. Madison saw the Bill as being redundant; but redundancy on a topic such as liberty and freedom was OK with him. In the end, Madison was OK with the Bill of Rights.

These amendments, known as the Bill of Rights were specific rights to be granted to citizens even if they had not conceived they already had the rights simply because the Constitution granted no such rights to government.

The Bill of Rights in summary explicitly limits the Federal government's powers, protects the rights of the people by preventing Congress from abridging freedom of speech, freedom of the press, freedom of assembly, freedom of religious worship, and the right to bear arms, and many others as noted in these ten specific amendments.

For example, the Bill of Rights prevents unreasonable search and seizure, cruel and unusual punishment, and self-incrimination, and it guarantees due process of law and a speedy public trial with an impartial jury.

In addition, the Bill of Rights states that "the enumeration in the Constitution, of certain rights, shall not be construed to deny or disparage others (rights) retained by the people," and reserves all powers not specifically granted to the Federal government to the citizenry or States. The original Ten Amendments to the Constitution, The Bill of Rights was introduced by Madison and passed by Congress September 25, 1789. These amendments came into effect when three/fourths of the states ratified them on December 15, 1791—four years after the Constitution had been created.

Chapter 18   Constitutional Problems of 2009-2016

Documented violations of law by President Obama and his administration

A number of respectable pundits and political writers have noted that President Obama, either by himself or through his administration—which he controls 100%, has not been faithful to his oath of office to execute faithfully the laws of the nation. They suggest that he has created legislation, a power reserved for the Legislative Branch, and that he has failed to execute laws that he swore to uphold. I can remember no president in my lifetime or in the history books who has rendered such callous disregard to the Constitution and the rights of the citizens of the United States.

Let's take a look at about thirteen of these compiled by the Committee for Justice in 2014, in no specific order. There are enough overall to create a whole new book for dummmies on this topic alone. There may be as few as 25 law violations or several hundred depending on who is watching. Here are some representative examples of Obama lawlessness:

1. Obama Administration used IRS to target conservative, Christian and pro-Israel organizations, donors, and citizens.
2. Justice Department ordered criminal investigations of FOX News reporters for doing their jobs during the 2012 election year.
3. President Obama, throughout his presidency, has refused to enforce long-established U.S.

immigration laws. For example (A.) the President stopped over 300,000 deportations and ordered the U.S. border patrol to release many of these illegal aliens in violation of law and without explanation. (B) Congress had overwhelmingly rejected Obama's so called DREAM ACT, so the President illegally enacted his own version of the DREAM ACT by Executive Order, permitting illegal aliens under 30 years of age to stay in America. (C.) The President consistently refused to build a double-barrier security fence along the U.S.-Mexican border in direct violation of the 2006 Secure Fence Act. Americans are wondering what happened to the fence. Ask the president.

4. The president continues an unconstitutional assault on our Second Amendment Right to Keep and Bear Arms. In one day, he issued 21 separate orders that attack and undermine the Second Amendment right to keep and bear arms.

5. The President has waged a war and has led an assault on Christians and religious freedom. HHS has, on the President's authority, without the approval of the Congress, demands that all health insurance plans must include coverage for abortion-inducing drugs. As a result, pro-life employers and taxpayers are now effectively required by law to pay for abortions. This mandate is an unconstitutional attack on the protections for freedom of religion and freedom of conscience in the First Amendment and the 1993 Religious Freedom Restoration Act.

6. The president forced ObamaCare on an unwilling public through bribery and lying about its cost. You may recall that he secured passage of ObamaCare by one vote in the Senate by bribing senators. He bribed Senator Ben Nelson of Nebraska with the notorious "Cornhusker Kickback." He bribed Senator Mary Landrieu with the infamous $300 million "Louisiana Purchase." In addition, Obama knowingly and blatantly lied to America and to

Congress about how much ObamaCare would really cost.

7. The President's Federal Communications Commission (FCC) chose to defy a court order and regulated the Internet. In other words, the President chose to go against the courts.

8. The Environmental Protection Agency (EPA) imposed Cross-State Air Pollution Rules on the state of Texas at the last minute and without an opportunity for Texas to respond to the proposed regulation. The EPA lied.

9. In violation of 10th Amendment, the president's Department of Justice (DOJ) violated State's rights by suing the State of Arizona from using reasonable measures to discourage illegal immigration within its borders

10. Without Congressional approval, Obama gutted the work requirement for welfare recipients passed by Congress and signed into law by President Bill Clinton.

11. In the bailout of General Motors and Chrysler, Obama illegally shortchanged bond holders in favor of Labor Unions, despite U.S. bankruptcy laws that specify that bond holders be first in line to be paid back.

12. Eager to use the killing of Osama bin Laden for political gain, the President exposed the identity and method of operation of the Navy SEALs team that conducted the operation in Pakistan, thus exposing its members to a lifetime of risk because they have been targeted for assassination by Islamists. A short time after Obama exposed the Navy SEALs' method of operation, 22 SEALs were shot down and killed in Afghanistan. It is a violation of law for the President or any American to reveal classified military secrets.

13. The President knowingly lied to Congress and the American people about the killing of U.S. Ambassador Chris Stevens and three other

Americans in Benghazi, Libya. The President and his representatives repeatedly said an anti-Islamic video sparked a spontaneous uprising in Libya that resulted in the killings even though Obama knew that the attack was a well-planned military-style assault by al Qaeda on the anniversary of September 11.

14. The First Lady's family trip to Africa in June of 2011, including a private safari at a South African game reserve, cost American taxpayers $424,000 for air travel alone. Mrs. Obama brought along both her makeup artist and hairstylist, as well as her mother, a niece and nephew, and her daughters, who were listed as "senior staff members." Are they legitimate staff members? Is this right? Is this against the law? You bet it is!

It would be nice if this were all. Rather than merely tell you that the president has behaved in a lawless fashion, with unauthorized changes to many laws including Obamacare seventy-one times, I presented the sampling above, courtesy of the committee for Justice, a Constitutional Watchdog. My goal is to make all the readers of this book Constitutional Watchdogs so that no employee of the people, from Congress to the Judges, to the President can choose to ignore the law of the people, the US Constitution with its accompanying Bill of Rights for the people.

Chapter 19   The Text of The Bill of Rights

A Charter of Freedom

The Bill of Rights is seen as the third of the three charters of freedom—the pillars of our Republic. Along with the Declaration of Independence and the Constitution, the Bill of Rights defines America. The Bill was granted by the Congress of the United States, begun and held at the City of New-York, on Wednesday the fourth of March, one thousand seven hundred and eighty nine.

The text of the Bill looks exactly as follows:

THE Conventions of a number of the States, having at the time of their adopting the Constitution, expressed a desire, in order to prevent misconstruction or abuse of its powers, that further declaratory and restrictive clauses should be added; And as extending the ground of public confidence in the Government, will best ensure the beneficent ends of its institution.

RESOLVED by the Senate and House of Representatives of the United States of America, in Congress assembled, two thirds of both Houses concurring, that the following Articles be proposed to the Legislatures of the several States, as amendments to the Constitution of the United States, all, or any of which Articles, when ratified by three-fourths of the said Legislatures, to be valid to all intents and purposes, as part of the said Constitution; viz.

ARTICLES in addition to, and Amendment of the Constitution of the United States of America, proposed by Congress, and ratified by the Legislatures of the several States, pursuant to the fifth Article of the original Constitution.

Article the first. *... After the first enumeration required by the first article of the Constitution, there shall be one Representative for every 30,000 until the number shall amount to 100, after which the proportion shall be so regulated by Congress, that there shall be not less than 100 Representatives, nor less than one Representative for every 40,000 persons, until the number of Representatives shall amount to 200; after which the proportion shall be so regulated by Congress, that there shall not be less than 200 Representatives, nor more than one Representative for every 50,000 persons.*

Article the second *... No law, varying the compensation for the services of the Senators and Representatives, shall take effect, until an election of Representatives shall have intervened.*

Article the third *... Congress shall make no law respecting an establishment of religion, or prohibiting the free exercise thereof; or abridging the freedom of speech, or of the press; or the right of the people peaceably to assemble, and to petition the Government for a redress of grievances.*

Article the fourth *... A well regulated Militia, being necessary to the security of a free state, the right of the people to keep and bear arms, shall not be infringed.*

Article the fifth *... No soldier shall, in time of peace be quartered in any house, without the consent of the owner, nor in time of war, but in a manner to be prescribed by law.*

Article the sixth ... *The right of the people to be secure in their persons, houses, papers, and effects, against unreasonable searches and seizures, shall not be violated, and no Warrants shall issue, but upon probable cause, supported by Oath or affirmation, and particularly describing the place to be searched, and the persons or things to be seized.*

Article the seventh ... *No person shall be held to answer for a capital, or otherwise infamous crime, unless on a presentment or indictment of a Grand Jury, except in cases arising in the land or naval forces, or in the Militia, when in actual service in time of war or public danger; nor shall any person be subject for the same offence to be twice put in jeopardy of life or limb; nor shall be compelled in any criminal case to be a witness against himself, nor be deprived of life, liberty, or property, without due process of law; nor shall private property be taken for public use, without just compensation.*

Article the eighth ... *In all criminal prosecutions, the accused shall enjoy the right to a speedy and public trial, by an impartial jury of the State and district wherein the crime shall have been committed, which district shall have been previously ascertained by law, and to be informed of the nature and cause of the accusation; to be confronted with the witnesses against him; to have compulsory process for obtaining witnesses in his favor, and to have the Assistance of Counsel for his defense.*

Article the ninth … *In suits at common law, where the value in controversy shall exceed twenty dollars, the right of trial by jury shall be preserved, and no fact tried by a jury, shall be otherwise re-examined in any Court of the United States, than according to the rules of the common law.*

Article the tenth *... Excessive bail shall not be required, nor excessive fines imposed, nor cruel and unusual punishments inflicted.*

Article the eleventh *.... The enumeration in the Constitution, of certain rights, shall not be construed to deny or disparage others retained by the people.*

Article the twelfth *... The powers not delegated to the United States by the Constitution, nor prohibited by it to the States, are reserved to the States respectively, or to the people."*

ATTEST,

Frederick Augustus Muhlenberg Speaker of the House of Representatives

John Adams, Vice-President of the United States, and President of the Senate.

John Beckley, Clerk of the House of Representatives. Sam A. Otis, Secretary of the Senate.

This work is in the public domain in the United States because it is a work of the United States

One more fact on the Bill of Rights is essential. The "Bill of Rights" is actually the popular name for a joint resolution passed by the first U.S. Congress on September 25, 1789.

The resolution proposed the first set of twelve amendments to the Constitution. Then as now, the process of amending the Constitution required that the resolution be "ratified" or approved by at least three quarters of the states.

Unlike the 10 amendments we know and cherish today as the Bill of Rights, the resolution sent to the states for ratification in 1789, proposed twelve amendments, not just ten. Knowing this body of law consists of just ten amendments, we therefore know that two were not ratified.

When the votes came in, from the 11 states that participated, on December 15, 1791, only the last 10 of the 12 amendments submitted had been ratified. And, so as you scour the original amendments looking for familiar text as in the First Amendment, you will have to cast your eyes to the third amendment proposed to find the contents of the first amendment as ratified.

Thus, the original third amendment, establishing freedom of speech, press, assembly, petition, and the right to a fair and speedy trial became today's First Amendment. Yet, when originally proposed, it was listed as the third amendment.

Chapter 20   Another look at the First Ten Constitutional Amendments

Greater than the Constitution???

To make sure we have the concept well understood, post facto, we offer another rationale for the Bill of Rights.

The Bill of Rights is the first thing most people think about when they think about the Constitution. In the Bill of Rights, a number of rights are specifically listed though they are already granted implicitly by the Constitution itself. The fundamental rights include freedom of the press, freedom of speech, freedom of religion and other wonderful freedoms that no people in any other country had ever enjoyed until the Founders and Framers christened America.

When the Constitution was ratified on March 4, 1789, it was because several states that held out would not go along until they knew a bill of rights for US citizens was in the cards. Many were concerned that they had given up rights that they already had as written in the Articles of Confederation.

Therefore, the Congress put together twelve amendments, which we have already examined, to satisfy their needs. Most were worked on by James Madison, who ironically was OK with the bare Constitution with no Bill of Rights. Ten of these bills passed / were ratified and two were rejected.

On December 15, 1791, the ten articles in the Bill of Rights were ratified, making these first ten changes part of the US Constitution. Any book about the Constitution must consider all of the debate and the finality of the Bill of Rights. Likewise any book about the Bill of rights must include the full scope of the Constitution.

So, now we say that the first ten constitutional amendments are known collectively as The Bill of Rights. They amplify freedoms for Americans that are and will always be included in the Constitution itself. Yet, in the new millennium America, the way many in government trample on these lifelines to freedom; one would think they were optional and that the framers cared nothing about them. Yet, this is not the case.

They are not optional. Any amendment becomes part of the overall law of the land, irrevocable by Congress, the President, or the Supreme Court. It is tough to overturn something as unconstitutional, when it actually is part of the Constitution.

Despite all the work in assuring freedom for all people, many otherwise intelligent Americans today choose not to understand their hard earned constitutional freedoms. This has permitted and continues to permit the knaves, such as the corrupt politicians in the government, and their backers—the socialist progressive Marxist/communists, to handily be taking our rights away. We must stop this encroachment on our liberties before it is too late.

The Bill of Rights may be the key to liberty and freedom, but the Constitution is the lock that shuts government out when it attempts to rule over the people for its own purposes. The Declaration of Independence, The Constitution and The Bill of Rights are intended to make the people supreme and the government subservient.

As we have studied, the US constitutional system consists of the power relationships among the principal branches of government resulting from the constitutional division and distribution of political authority among them by the Constitution itself.

It defines the roles in the governing process played by each of the principal governmental institutions defined within the Constitution. Americans must understand this in order to protect their personal freedoms. I hope that is why you chose to read The Bill of Rights 4 Dummmies! You may also find that The Constitution 4 Dummmies!, another Lets Go Publish! Book will help your studies. www.bookhawkers.com

It is easy to be swayed when your source of news is the corrupt popular media, who, from recent accounts would like there to be no Constitution and they would be fine if the people had no means of protecting their inalienable rights. So, the message from this author is to be careful!

This notion is very important for Americans in that the Constitution provides the following attributes of government on our behalf:

- Divides and distributes the authority of government between the central government over the whole nation and the governments of the member-states of the federal union
- Assigns certain governmental powers to the states, while denying them certain other powers
- Assigns certain powers to the national government and expressly prohibits it from exercising any powers not explicitly granted. ----- In other words, the Federal government cannot by law decide that you cannot use anything. For example, they have unlawfully decreed you cannot use incandescent light bulbs as those invented by Thomas Edison. When the government is permitted to do things like this that violate personal freedom, it is operating outside of its constitutional authority. Since Congress has permitted this and similar erosions of the people's power, your author suggests that we all call our congressional

representatives home and replace them with a set of
people who are not afraid to represent the real
interests of the people.
- Assigns the powers delegated to the national
government to the principal entities of that
government (The U.S. House of Representatives, the
U.S. Senate, the President of the U.S.A., and the U.S.
Courts system, with supreme judicial power reserved
for the Supreme Court). Each entity has its own
power, a strong incentive, and a legal right to oppose,
block, check, and restrain the other entities of
government when they get off track.
- Prescribes certain limitations on both the central
government and the states by guaranteeing civil
liberties, i.e., the basic rights and liberties of the
individual citizen.

Facets of the constitutionality of the government may be
overridden in fact if not in deed. As noted previously in this
text, the current President has chosen to ignore Congress and
to not follow the Constitution as the explicit enforcer of the
law in America. In many ways, we are having a
constitutional crisis today and our leaders, the politicians we
elect, do not seem up to the task of defending the Bill of
Rights and the Constitution. This is a big problem.

The Congress, choosing to be an inept body for several years
prior to and including 2014, enabled the President's power
grab through inaction—though it remains unconstitutional.

Power abuse will continue until the people (US) vote out all
members of the assembly who are in line with the ideology of
a lawless president. The US government must comply with
two fundamental legal requirements to remain legitimate

— The government must operate in accordance with the
provisions of the Constitution
— The government must not exceed the authority granted to
it by the Constitution.

The bottom line unfortunately for all Americans is that our government can be declared illegitimate since it complies with neither of these requirements. Check the news sources. Check the blogs. Check the White House logs. This Administration points its middle finger at the Constitution and that makes the government illegitimate. See the two provisions above.

As much as we may personally like our representatives, we do not want them taking more power than we are willing to give them. When you read the Constitution, it is clear how insightful the Founding Fathers were as they built the essential features of constitutionalism into the framework of the US government. The government's compliance with these two basic legal requirements is essential to its legitimacy.

Government can do as it may choose if unchecked. The people must checkmate the government by sending reputable, non-politicians to represent US.

So if we were to summarize the central purpose of constitutionalism in 2014 / 2015, it would begin by sounding like this.

> *It is to protect ourselves from our too-far-reaching neighbors who become politicians to promote their own welfare.*

The notion of limiting governmental power as dictated in the Constitution checks and restrains the persons who hold public office and who exercise political authority.

Thus, it is up to all of US as a wary and watchful society that our otherwise wonderful government does not get out of control. Hopefully, this book will help US all in this regard. America is not supposed to be a place for dummmies. It is a place where all people are given the opportunity to be the best and the brightest. Our Constitution and the Bill of Rights assure this.

These historic documents, the Constitution of our wonderful union of states, and its companion Bill of Rights has protected us for so long (well over 225 years) that we take it for granted. Progressive, aka communist leaders on the left in the USA, hoping we are all dummmies are plotting to rob US of our inalienable rights so they can add to their wallets, and their personal opportunities. If they cared as much about We the People, as they do about their own interests, America would be a far better place in which to live.

The first constitutional battle

Like all good stories, the more times you hear them, the more believable they becomes. This story is that of the need for the Bill of Rights and the Constitution, with a recap of the battle to achieve both. Some patriots were for a Bill of Rights and some patriots were not. It is a battle worth reexamining.

Just a few years after the Constitution was written and approved by the convention, a new political battle had ensued. It pitted the Founding Fathers against one another and threatened the ratification of the document over which they'd wrestled so hard and long to create.

The Federalists, major patriots, as noted in this and prior chapters, including James Madison, George Washington and Alexander Hamilton, feared that if some rights were listed, others not explicitly enumerated would be left vulnerable.

On the other side, another group of major patriots, known as the Anti-federalists, included George Mason, Thomas Jefferson and Patrick Henry. This group was adamant that the Constitution must explicitly guarantee certain fundamental rights that no government could take away.

They believed that not listing rights risked there being no rights.

Out of it all, all twelve notions brought forward to the Congress to be included in the Bill of Rights were approved and later just ten were ratified by the states. The Bill of Rights is a hallmark of our Democratic Republic, and never were so many Constitutional Amendments approved by the Congress of the US and ratified by the states in such short order

In the end, we have the US Constitution!

At the end of the Constitutional Convention in 1789, Benjamin Franklin, a great Founder from Pennsylvania, wrote:

"It is a singular thing in the history of mankind that a great people have had the opportunity of forming a government for themselves. We are making experiment in politics. In these sentiments, I agree to this Constitution, with all its faults, if they are such. For when you assemble a number of men to have the advantage of their joint wisdom, you inevitably assemble with those men all their prejudices, their passions, their errors of opinion, their local interests, and their selfish views. It therefore astonishes me to find this system approaching so near to perfection as it does."

Franklin also warned, "We must all hang together, or most assuredly we shall all hang separately." But, admittedly, this comment was made before the Revolutionary War!

Chapter 21   Summary of All Proposed Constitutional Amendments

Can such great works be summarized?

Without reading the full text of an amendment, one cannot gain its full impact on the freedoms and rights of American citizens. Even then, for average Joe's, such verbiage is tough to read.

Though the amendments to the Constitution can be summarized, it is for purposes other than understanding their full impact on the nation. It is for a perspective on what they contain from cover to cover without having to read all between. Like all summaries, citizens get to read about the nature and the planned purposes of the amendments even without reading them. So, summaries do have value.

The summaries do not give the notion of the full text of the principles of our government for sure but they show where correction was needed and applied. The Founders admitted that they were imperfect. All humans are imperfect. So, when the Founders created the Articles of Confederation to govern the United States, it was round one of an effort to make a more perfect democratic republic.

As humans, after a time, even the Founders doubted the perfection of their resulting work. No human delivers perfection ever—only God. So, should the founders have given up and said c'est la vie (French for that's just how it is)—when the Articles of Confederation were deemed imperfect? Should they have gone home, opened up a bottle of the finest wine and approved of themselves to the bottom of the bottle. Or should they have taken another try to do better? Of course, we all vote for the latter and so did the Founders.

There is nothing like the original and that is why in preceding chapters we discuss the Constitution as written, prior to the Bill of Rights. The Bill of Rights certainly has helped the hoi polloi and the hoity-toity understand this major historical document far better.

In the appendices of this book, there is much text which further explains the position of the Bill of Rights in context with the US Constitution. The Constitution improved on the Articles of Confederation, and the Bill of Rights clarified for the common man, a number of key rights inherent in the Constitution.

The Bill of Rights has been fully explained in their purpose and their meaning in this and preceding chapters of this book. It is a feel good document for scholars but it is an essential document for Americans searching for just a few well written sentences describing their rights.

The Bill of Rights changed the Constitution to make it clear that Americans had specific rights, not just those denied to the federal government through the Constitution. The US government, over the next two hundred plus years from the Constitution's ratification found just seventeen additional changes to the Constitution necessary once the Bill of Rights became the first ten amendments.

These of course were in addition to the ten amendments (changes) already included in the Bill of Rights. These twenty-seven amendments make the US Constitution an even better, and an even more perfect union of the United States of America than the Constitution alone, when it replaced the Articles of Confederation.

Let's take a quick snapshot of the entire twenty-seven Amendments including the first ten, the Bill of Rights. Besides the Constitution itself, these are the outward principles upon which our freedoms and our liberties are cast.

The Bill of Rights in summary:

— **Amendment I:** Freedom of speech, religion, press, petition, assembly.
— **Amendment II:** Right to bear arms and militia.
— **Amendment III**: Quartering of soldiers.
— **Amendment IV:** Warrants and searches.
— **Amendment V:** Individual debt and double jeopardy.
— **Amendment VI:** Speedy trial, witnesses and accusations.
— **Amendment VII:** Right for a jury trial.
— **Amendment VIII:** Bail and fines.
— **Amendment IX**: Existence of other rights for the people
— **Amendment X:** Power reserved to the states and people.

Later amendments in summary

— **Amendment XI:** Suits against states.
— **Amendment XII:** Election of executive branch.
— **Amendment XIII:** Prohibition of slavery.
— **Amendment XIV:** Privileges or immunities, due process, elections and debt: Consists of 5 sections and defines: (1) Citizenship (2) Apportionment of representatives among the states, (3) Rules for being a senator or representative, (4) Validity of the public debt, (5) Congressional enforcement of this Article.
— **Amendment XV:** Race and the right to vote.
— **Amendment XVI:** US Income tax enabled.
— **Amendment XVII:** Senator election change and number.
— **Amendment XVIII:** Prohibition on sale of alcohol

- **Amendment XIX:** Gender and the right to vote.
- **Amendment XX:** "Lame duck" Congress eliminated.
- **Amendment XXI:** Repeal of Amendment XVIII (Prohibition).
- **Amendment XXII:** Limit of Presidential terms.
- **Amendment XXIII:** Election rules for the District of Columbia
- **Amendment XXIV:** Taxes and the right to vote.
- **Amendment XXV:** Rules of Presidential succession.
- **Amendment XXVI:** Age and the right to vote.
- **Amendment XXVII:** Pay raises and Congress

Amendments Never Ratified

Besides the above summary of the constitutional body of law, six other amendments have been proposed to the Constitution that have not been ratified and thus do not represent the law of the land. The entire text of these amendments is included in Appendix G.

The original first amendment was never ratified. It set the ratio of representatives of Congress to constituents. If this amendment had made it to the bill of Rights, and been ratified, the number of members of the House of Representatives could by now be over 6,000, compared to the present 435. As apportioned by the 2000 Census, each member of the House currently represents about 650,000 people.

The original second amendment passed by Congress which was not ratified, was eventually ratified as the 27th amendment of the United States 203 years after it was first offered. It has to do with Congressional Salaries.

What does all this mean?

We have examined the founding and the revolution and the articles and precepts in the Constitution as the primary law of the land. We have also examined the Bill of rights in detail and the other amendments to the Constitution in summary form.

For you, as you have read this material, you are a member of a more informed electorate. When you get the government you deserve, because you care about America and you are learning more and more about your country, when you get the government you deserve, it can be a much better government.

Chapter 22   The Federalist Papers

The Constitution—great but not perfect!

Most Americans already know that our nation today is in peril; yet many Americans choose not to believe this is the case. For those who see it as it is, tyranny in our highest federal offices, it would help for all of US to do as you are doing with this book. Reread the Declaration of Independence and the Constitution, and the Bill of Rights. We have examined each of these historical documents in detail in this book. And so all readers—at this point of this book—especially those who have read the Appendices—are already qualified to see the current goings-on, as pure tyranny.

Would the Founders have expected this? To know more about what was on the minds of the Founders when they put forth this great Constitution, and the Bill of Rights, there is a real way in which we can almost crawl into the pure minds of our Founders.

As you have learned so far, the Founders and the Constitution Framers never expected corruption to interfere with the many checks and balances they had prepared for America and had written into the Constitution and the Bill of Rights. Yet, here we are, we have a lawless and lying presidential administration and tyranny that we have not seen since England was our master. To make matters worse, we have a Congress full of wimps, who will not assure the Law of the Land.

To know what the founders thought in the 1780's when all of the great ideas were flowing, it helps to read The Federalist Papers, a series of 85 essays written by Alexander Hamilton, John Jay, and James Madison. They explain the thought process on all aspects of the Constitution. Let's Go Publish (LGP) has a new edition of the Federalist Papers that uses the same words but with shorter paragraphs, making the papers far easier to read. It is available at www.bookhawkers.com. You can preview this book at www.bookhawkers.com. By reading the Federalist Papers you will better understand the Constitution.

You do not have to buy this book, however, to enjoy these masterpiece essays. The Federalist Papers are free on the Internet. For example, you can read the entire set of The Federalist Papers online. The following URL is excellent: http://www.constitution.org/fed/federa00.htm

Glenn Beck on his show just this morning in July, 2014 suggested that the Constitution is a gift from God. They indeed are just that. The Federalist Papers are a means of understanding this document more than otherwise possible.

Back in 1787, a number of states had sent detailed written plans for the Constitution along with their delegates to the Constitutional Convention in Philadelphia. The Convention began on May 25, 1787 and lasted until September 17, 1787. On September 17, 1787, the state delegates approved the Constitution as written by Madison et al in its final form. The Framers had completed their work and sent the document back to the individual states to be ratified. They then adjourned the convention. Without ratification, however, the Constitution was not yet the law of the land.

Convincing the Public

The commencing of the Federalist Papers began shortly thereafter. The writing of the papers was commissioned by Alexander Hamilton, a great patriot, who knew he could not write all of the arguments necessary for the people to choose to agree to back the Constitution. Hamilton, and James Madison, and John Jay together wrote The Federalist Papers to defend and explain the newly drafted Federal Constitution, and to promote its ratification in the state of New York. A group of folks just as patriotic but who were dead-set against the Constitution became known as the Anti-Federalists.

Each of the papers was written as an essay, but when published they became articles in New York newspapers and magazines. Because New York at the time and to this day is a huge and prosperous state, their being published in NY was very important for the ratification of the Constitution. Thus for the writers, it was the major objective of their attention at the time.

The Federalist Papers, written by Alexander Hamilton, John Jay, and James Madison answered the debated questions as posed by the opposition in great detail while copious detractors wrote their own essays / articles in rebuttal. As noted above, and worth repeating, the opposition articles collectively are known as the Anti-Federalist Papers.

Many were published in the press so as to offer other thoughts on such an important issue.

Nowhere was the furor over the proposed Constitution in the few states of the US more intense than in New York. Governor George Clinton was very concerned that the state's influence would be compromised at the Constitutional Convention.

The NY Legislature selected State Supreme Court Judge Robert Yates and John Lansing, Speaker of the NY Assembly; to attend the convention. Both were well known Anti-Federalists. Their selection was seen by many as a way for New York to be able to outvote Alexander Hamilton.

There were those, such as Yates and Lansing, whose opposition to the new document was based on their view that the Constitution diminished the rights that Americans had won in the Revolution. The Federalist Papers presented a view that this was not true while the Anti-Federalist Papers, also displayed in popular newspapers of the day, presented a view that the Constitution was bad for America and offered its specific notions.

Alexander Hamilton became fearful that the cause for the Constitution might be lost in his home state of New York. And to be repetitive for learning purposes, this was his purpose in putting together the Federalist Papers.

Hamilton published his first "Federalist" essay in the New York Independent Journal on October 27, 1787

The Federalist, also called *The Federalist Papers*, has served two very different purposes in American history. The 85 essays succeeded in helping to persuade doubtful New Yorkers (as well as the public in the other states), despite the well written efforts of the Anti-Federalists, to ratify the Constitution.

Today, The Federalist Papers help the rest of US to more clearly understand what the writers of the Constitution had in mind when they drafted this amazing document more than 225 years ago.

"America- if we cannot define Liberty, we cannot defend it. If we cannot define tyranny, we cannot defeat it- "KrisAnne Hall
www.conservativeactionalerts.com/author/krisanne-hall

"If a nation expects to be ignorant and free, in a state of civilization, it expects what never was and never will be."
- Thomas Jefferson

Let us all be smart. Let us pay attention, and let us continue to be free with unlimited liberty in the finest country that God ever permitted being founded.

Appendix A: The Declaration of Rights and Grievances

At the First Continental Congress, the delegates drafted several documents, and several drafts of documents, one of which was the Declaration of Rights and Grievances. This was a statement of American complaints. It was sent to King George III, to whom, at the time, many of the delegates remained loyal. It was not sent to Parliament since the delegates did not have the same level of loyalty to this body. Quite frankly, The document implored King George III to step in and rescue the colonies from the English Parliament.

The radical delegates were critical of this particular Declaration because it continued to concede the right of Parliament to regulate colonial trade, a view that was losing favor in the mid-1770s. Many suggest that the actual cause of the American Revolution is found in this major historical document.

The full text of the Declaration of Rights and Grievances is displayed in this Appendix.

THUS, IN THE FIRST CONTINENTAL CONGRESS, WHICH MET IN SEPTEMBER AND OCTOBER 1774, THE DELEGATES OF THE CONGRESS MADE SEVERAL MAJOR DECISIONS. AMONG THOSE WAS TO SEND KING GEORGE III THIS DECLARATION OF RIGHTS AND GRIEVANCES, WHICH IS SHOWN BELOW: .

In Congress, at Philadelphia, October 14, 1774

Whereas, since the close of the last war, the British Parliament, claiming a power of right to bind the people of America, by statute, all cases whatsoever, hath in some acts expressly imposed taxes on them and in others, under various pretenses, but in fact for the purpose raising a revenue, hath imposed rates and duties payable in these colonies established a board of commissioners, with unconstitutional powers, and extended the jurisdiction of courts of admiralty, not only for collecting the said duties, but for the trial of causes merely arising within the body of a county.

And whereas, in consequence of other statutes, judges, who before held only estates at will in their offices, have been made dependent on the Crown alone for their salaries, and standing armies kept in time of peace:

And whereas, it has lately been resolved in Parliament, that by force of a statute, made in the thirty-fifth year of the reign of Henry the Eighth, colonists may be transported to England, and tried there upon accusations for treasons, and misprisions, or concealments of treasons committed in the colonies, and by a late statute, such trials have been directed in cases therein mentioned.

And whereas, in the last session of Parliament, three statutes were made; one, entitled "An act to discontinue, in such manner and for such time as are therein mentioned, the landing and discharging, lading, or shipping of goods, wares and merchandise, at the town, and within the harbor of Boston, in the province of Massachusetts Bay, in North America"; and another, entitled "An act for the better regulating the government of the province of the Massachusetts Bay in New England"; and another, entitled "An act for the impartial administration of justice, in the cases of persons questioned for any act done by them in the execution of the law, or for the suppression of riots and tumults in the province of the Massachusetts Bay, in New England." And another statute was then made, "for making more effectual provision for the government of the province of Quebec, etc." All which statutes are impolitic, unjust and cruel, as well as unconstitutional, and most dangerous and destructive of American rights.

And whereas, assemblies have been frequently dissolved, contrary to the rights of the people, when they attempted to deliberate on grievances; and their dutiful, humble, loyal, and reasonable petitions to the Crown for redress, have been repeatedly treated with contempt by His Majesty's ministers of state:

The good people of the several colonies of New Hampshire, Massachusetts Bay, Rhode Island and Providence Plantations, Connecticut, New York, New Jersey, Pennsylvania, New Castle, Kent and Sussex on Delaware, Maryland, Virginia, North Carolina, and South Carolina, justly alarmed at these arbitrary proceedings of Parliament and administration, have severally elected, constituted, and appointed deputies to meet and sit in general congress, in the city of Philadelphia, in order to obtain such establishment, as that their religion, laws, and liberties may not be subverted.

Whereupon the deputies so appointed being now assembled, in a full and free representation of these colonies, taking into their most serious consideration, the best means of attaining the ends aforesaid, do, in the first place, as Englishmen, their ancestors in like cases have usually done, for asserting and vindicating their rights and liberties, declare,

That the inhabitants of the English colonies in North America, by the immutable laws of nature, the principles of the English Constitution, and the several charters or compacts, have the following rights:

1. That they are entitled to life, liberty, and property, and they have never ceded to any sovereign power whatever, a right to dispose of either without their consent.

2. That our ancestors, who first settled these colonies, were at the time of their emigration from the mother country, entitled to all the rights, liberties, and immunities of free and natural-born subjects, within the realm of England.

3. That by such emigration they by no means forfeited, surrendered, or lost any of those rights, but that they were, and their descendants now are, entitled to the exercise and enjoyment of all such of them, as their local and other circumstances enable them, to exercise and enjoy.

4. That the foundation of English liberty, and of all free government, is a right in the people to participate in their legislative council: and as the English colonists are not represented, and from their local and other circumstances, can not properly be represented in the British Parliament, they are entitled to a free and exclusive power of legislation in their several provincial legislatures, where their right of representation can alone be preserved, in all cases of taxation and internal polity, subject only to the negative of their sovereign, in such manner as has been heretofore used and accustomed. But, from the necessity of the case, and a regard to the mutual interest of both countries, we cheerfully consent to the operation of such acts of the British Parliament, as are bona fide, restrained to the regulation of our external commerce, for the purpose of securing the commercial advantages of the whole empire to the mother country, and the commercial benefits of its respective members; excluding every idea of taxation, internal or eternal, for raising a revenue on the subjects in America, without their consent.

5. That the respective colonies are entitled to the common law of England, and more especially to the great and inestimable privilege of being tried by their peers of the vicinage, according to the course of that law.

6. That they are entitled to the benefit of such of the English statutes as existed at the time of their colonization; and which they have, by experience, respectively found to be applicable to their several local and other circumstances.

7. That these, His Majesty's colonies, are likewise entitled to all the immunities and privileges granted and confirmed to them by royal charters, or secured by their several codes of provincial laws.

8. That they have a right peaceably to assemble, consider of their grievances, and petition the King; and that all prosecutions, prohibitory proclamations, and commitment for the same, are illegal.

9. That the keeping a standing army in these colonies, in times of peace, without the consent of the legislature of that colony, in which such army is kept, is against law.

10. It is indispensably necessary to good government, and rendered essential by the English constitution, that the constituent branches of the legislature be independent of each other; that, therefore, the exercise of legislative power in several colonies, by a council appointed, during pleasure by the Crown, is unconstitutional, dangerous, and destructive to the freedom of American legislation.

All and each of which the aforesaid deputies, in behalf of themselves and their constituents, do claim, demand, and insist on, as their indubitable rights and liberties; which can not be legally taken from them, altered or abridged by any power whatever, without their own consent, by their representatives in their several provincial legislatures.

In the course of our inquiry, we find many infringements and violations of the foregoing rights, which, from an ardent desire, that harmony and mutual intercourse of affection and interest may be restored, we pass over for the present, and proceed to state such acts and measures as have been adopted since the last war, which demonstrate a system formed to enslave America.
Resolved, N. C. D. That the following acts of Parliament are infringements and violations of the rights of the colonists; and that the repeal of them is essentially necessary in order to restore harmony between Great Britain and the American colonies, viz;

The several acts of 4 Geo. 3. ch. 15, and ch. 34.--5 Geo. 3. ch. 25.--6 Geo. 3. ch. 52.--7 Geo. 3. ch. 41, and ch. 46.--8 Geo. 3. ch. 22, which impose duties for the purpose of raising a revenue in America, extend the powers of the admiralty court beyond their ancient limits, deprive the American subject of trial by jury, authorize the judges' certificate to indemnify the prosecutor from damages, that he might otherwise be liable to, requiring oppressive security from a claimant of ships and goods seized, before he shall be allowed to defend his property, and are subversive of American rights.

Also the 12 Geo. 3. ch. 24, entitled "An act for the better securing His Majesty's dock yards, magazines, ships, ammunition, and stores," which declares a new offense in America, and deprives the American subject of a constitutional trial by jury of the vicinage, by authorizing the trial of any person, charged with the committing any offense described in the said act, out of the realm, to be indicted and tried for the same in any shire or county within the realm.

Also the three acts passed in the last session of Parliament, for stopping the port and blocking up the harbor of Boston, for altering the charter and government of the Massachusetts Bay, and that which is entitled "An act for the better administration of justice," etc.

Also the act passed in the same session for establishing the Roman Catholic religion in the province of Quebec, abolishing the equitable system of English laws, and erecting a tyranny there, to the great danger, from so total a dissimilarity of religion, law, and government of the neighboring British colonies, by the assitance of whose blood and treasure the said country was conquered from France.

Also the act passed in the same session for the better providing suitable quarters for officers and soldiers in His Majesty's service in North America.

Also, that the keeping a standing army in several of these colonies, in time of peace, without the consent of the legislature of that colony in which such army is kept, is against law.

To these grievous acts and measures, Americans can not submit, but in hopes that their fellow subjects in Great Britain will, on a revision of them, restore us to that state in which both countries found happiness and prosperity, we have for the present only resolved to pursue the following peaceable measures:

1st. To enter into a non-importation, non-consumption, and non exportation agreement or association.

2. To prepare an address to the people of Great Britain, and a memorial to the inhabitants of British America, and

3. To prepare a loyal address to His Majesty; agreeable to resolutions already entered into

Appendix B: The Articles of Association

Articles of Association stated that if the Intolerable Acts were not repealed by December 1, 1774, a boycott of British goods would begin in the colonies. The full text of the Articles of Association is included in this Appendix.

--

The Articles of Association

October 20, 1774

We, his majesty's most loyal subjects, the delegates of the several colonies of New-Hampshire, Massachusetts-Bay, Rhode-Island, Connecticut, New-York, New-Jersey, Pennsylvania, the three lower counties of Newcastle, Kent and Sussex on Delaware, Maryland, Virginia, North-Carolina, and South-Carolina, deputed to represent them in a continental Congress, held in the city of Philadelphia, on the 5th day of September, 1774, avowing our allegiance to his majesty, our affection and regard for our fellow-subjects in Great-Britain and elsewhere, affected with the deepest anxiety, and most alarming apprehensions, at those grievances and distresses, with which his Majesty's American subjects are oppressed; and having taken under our most serious deliberation, the state of the whole continent, find, that the present unhappy situation of our affairs is occasioned by a ruinous system of colony administration, adopted by the British ministry about the year 1763, evidently calculated for enslaving these colonies, and, with them, the British Empire. In prosecution of which system, various acts of parliament have been passed, for raising a revenue in America, for depriving the American subjects, in many instances, of the constitutional trial by jury, exposing their lives to danger, by directing a new and illegal trial beyond the seas, for crimes alleged to have been committed in America: And in prosecution of the same system, several late, cruel, and oppressive acts have been passed, respecting the town of Boston and the Massachusetts-Bay, and also an act for extending the province of Quebec, so as to border on the western frontiers of these colonies, establishing an arbitrary government therein, and discouraging the settlement of British subjects in that wide extended country; thus, by the influence of civil principles and ancient prejudices, to dispose the inhabitants to act with hostility against the free Protestant colonies, whenever a wicked ministry shall choose so to direct them.

To obtain redress of these grievances, which threaten destruction to the lives liberty, and property of his majesty's subjects, in North-America, we are of opinion, that a non-importation, non-consumption, and non-exportation agreement, faithfully adhered to, will prove the most speedy, effectual, and peaceable measure: And, therefore, we do, for ourselves, and the inhabitants of the several colonies, whom we represent, firmly agree and associate, under the sacred ties of virtue, honour and love of our country, as follows:

1. That from and after the first day of December next, we will not import, into British America, from Great-Britain or Ireland, any goods, wares, or merchandise whatsoever, or from any other place, any such goods, wares, or merchandise, as shall have been exported from Great-Britain or Ireland; nor will we, after that day, import any East-India tea from any part of the world; nor any molasses, syrups, paneles, coffee, or pimento, from the British plantations or from Dominica; nor wines from Madeira, or the Western Islands; nor foreign indigo.

2. We will neither import nor purchase, any slave imported after the first day of December next; after which time, we will wholly discontinue the slave trade, and will neither be concerned in it ourselves, nor will we hire our vessels, nor sell our commodities or manufactures to those who are concerned in it.

3. As a non-consumption agreement, strictly adhered to, will be an effectual security for the observation of the non-importation, we, as above, solemnly agree and associate, that from this day, we will not purchase or use any tea, imported on account of the East-India company, or any on which a duty hath been or shall be paid; and from and after the first day of March next, we will not purchase or use any East-India tea whatever; nor will we, nor shall any person for or under us, purchase or use any of those goods, wares, or merchandise, we have agreed not to import, which we shall know, or have cause to suspect, were imported after the first day of December, except such as come under the rules and directions of the tenth article hereafter mentioned.

4. The earnest desire we have not to injure our fellow-subjects in Great-Britain, Ireland, or the West-Indies, induces us to suspend a non-exportation, until the tenth day of September, 1775; at which time, if the said acts and parts of acts of the British parliament herein after mentioned, are not repealed, we will not directly or indirectly, export any merchandise or commodity whatsoever to Great-Britain, Ireland, or the West-Indies, except rice to Europe.

5. Such as are merchants, and use the British and Irish trade, will give orders, as soon as possible, to their factors, agents and correspondents, in Great-Britain and Ireland, not to ship any goods to them, on any pretence whatsoever, as they cannot be received in America; and if any merchant, residing in Great-Britain or Ireland, shall directly or indirectly ship any goods, wares or merchandize, for America, in order to break the said non-importation agreement, or in any manner contravene the same, on such unworthy conduct being well attested, it ought to be made public; and, on the same being so done, we will not, from thenceforth, have any commercial connexion with such merchant.

6. That such as are owners of vessels will give positive orders to their captains, or masters, not to receive on board their vessels any goods prohibited by the said non-importation agreement, on pain of immediate dismission from their service.

7. We will use our utmost endeavours to improve the breed of sheep, and increase their number to the greatest extent; and to that end, we will kill them as seldom as may be, especially those of the most profitable kind; nor will we export any to the West-Indies or elsewhere; and those of us, who are or may become overstocked with, or can conveniently spare any sheep, will dispose of them to our neighbours, especially to the poorer sort, on moderate terms.

8. We will, in our several stations, encourage frugality, economy, and industry, and promote agriculture, arts and the manufactures of this country, especially that of wool; and will discountenance and discourage every species of extravagance and dissipation, especially all horse-racing, and all kinds of games, cock fighting, exhibitions of shews, plays, and other expensive diversions and entertainments; and on the death of any relation or friend, none of us, or any of our families will go into any further mourning-dress, than a black crepe or ribbon on the arm or hat, for gentlemen, and a black ribbon and necklace for ladies, and we will discontinue the giving of gloves and scarves at funerals.

9. Such as are venders of goods or merchandize will not take advantage of the scarcity of goods, that may be occasioned by this association, but will sell the same at the rates we have been respectively accustomed to do, for twelve months last past. -And if any vender of goods or merchandise shall sell such goods on higher terms, or shall, in any manner, or by any device whatsoever, violate or depart from this agreement, no person ought, nor will any of us deal with any such person, or his or her factor or agent, at any time thereafter, for any commodity whatever.

10. In case any merchant, trader, or other person, shall import any goods or merchandize, after the first day of December, and before the first day of February next, the same ought forthwith, at the election of the owner, to be either re-shipped or delivered up to the committee of the country or town, wherein they shall be imported, to be stored at the risque of the importer, until the non-importation agreement shall cease, or be sold under the direction of the committee aforesaid; and in the last-mentioned case, the owner or owners of such goods shall be reimbursed out of the sales, the first cost and charges, the profit, if any, to be applied towards relieving and employing such poor inhabitants of the town of Boston, as are immediate sufferers by the Boston port-bill; and a particular account of all goods so returned, stored, or sold, to be inserted in the public papers; and if any goods or merchandizes shall be imported after the said first day of February, the same ought forthwith to be sent back again, without breaking any of the packages thereof.

11. That a committee be chosen in every county, city, and town, by those who are qualified to vote for representatives in the legislature, whose business it shall be attentively to observe the conduct of all persons touching this association; and when it shall be made to appear, to the satisfaction of a majority of any such committee, that any person within the limits of their appointment has violated this association, that such majority do forthwith cause the truth of the case to be published in the gazette; to the end, that all such foes to the rights of British-America may be publicly known, and universally contemned as the enemies of American liberty; and thenceforth we respectively will break off all dealings with him or her.

12. That the committee of correspondence, in the respective colonies, do frequently inspect the entries of their customhouses, and inform each other, from time to time, of the true state thereof, and of every other material circumstance that may occur relative to this association.

13. That all manufactures of this country be sold at reasonable prices, so- that no undue advantage be taken of a future scarcity of goods.

14. And we do further agree and resolve that we will have no trade, commerce, dealings or intercourse whatsoever, with any colony or province, in North-America, which shall not accede to, or which shall hereafter violate this association, but will hold them as unworthy of the rights of freemen, and as inimical to the liberties of their country.

And we do solemnly bind ourselves and our constituents, under the ties aforesaid, to adhere to this association, until such parts of the several acts of parliament passed since the close of the last war, as impose or continue duties on tea, wine, molasses, syrups paneles, coffee, sugar, pimento, indigo, foreign paper, glass, and painters' colours, imported into America, and extend the powers of the admiralty courts beyond their ancient limits, deprive the American subject of trial by jury, authorize the judge's certificate to indemnify the prosecutor from damages, that he might otherwise be liable to from a trial by his peers, require oppressive security from a claimant of ships or goods seized, before he shall be allowed to defend his property, are repealed.-And until that part of the act of the 12 G. 3. ch. 24, entitled "An act for the better securing his majesty's dock-yards magazines, ships, ammunition, and stores," by which any persons charged with committing any of the offenses therein described, in America, may be tried in any shire or county within the realm, is repealed-and until the four acts, passed the last session of parliament, viz. that for stopping the port and blocking up the harbour of Boston-that for altering the charter and government of the Massachusetts-Bay-and that which is entitled "An act for the better administration of justice, &c."-and that "for extending the limits of Quebec, &c." are repealed. And we recommend it to the provincial conventions, and to the committees in the respective colonies, to establish such farther regulations as they may think proper, for carrying into execution this association.

The foregoing association being determined upon by the Congress, was ordered to be subscribed by the several members thereof; and thereupon, we have hereunto set our respective names accordingly.

IN CONGRESS, PHILADELPHIA, October 20, 1774.
PEYTON RANDOLPH, President.

New Hampshire :   John Sullivan, Nathaniel Folsom
Massachusetts Bay : Thomas Cushing, Samuel Adams, John Adams, Robert Treat Paine
Rhode Island: Stephen Hopkins, Samuel Ward
Connecticut: Eliphalet Dyer, Roger Sherman, Silas Deane
New York: Isaac Low, John Alsop, John Jay, James Duane, Philip Livingston, William Floyd, Henry Wisner, Simon. Boerum
New Jersey: James. Kinsey, William. Livingston, Stephen Crane, Richard. Smith, John De Hart
Pennsylvania: Joseph Galloway, John Dickinson , Charles Humphreys, Thomas Mifflin, Edward Biddle, John Morton, George Ross
The Lower Counties New Castle: Cæsar Rodney, Thomas. M: Kean, George Read
Maryland: Matthew Tilghman, Thomas Johnson Junior, William Paca, Samuel Chase
Virginia: Richard Henry Lee, George Washington, Patrick Henry, Junior, Richard Bland, Benjamin Harrison, Edmund Pendleton

North-Carolina: William Hooper, Joseph Hewes, Richard Caswell

South-Carolina: Henry Middleton, Thomas Lynch, Christopher Gadsden, John Rutledge, Edward Rutledge

Appendix C: The Declaration of Independence

On July 4, 1776, the Second Continental Congress, announced that the thirteen American colonies, then at war with Great Britain, regarded themselves as 13 newly independent sovereign states, and no longer a part of the British Empire. The full text of the Declaration of Independence is displayed in this Appendix.

IN CONGRESS, JULY 4, 1776

The Unanimous Declaration of the thirteen United States of America

When in the Course of human events it becomes necessary for one people to dissolve the political bands which have connected them with another and to assume among the powers of the earth, the separate and equal station to which the Laws of Nature and of Nature's God entitle them, a decent respect to the opinions of mankind requires that they should declare the causes which impel them to the separation.

We hold these truths to be self-evident, that all men are created equal, that they are endowed by their Creator with certain unalienable Rights, that among these are Life, Liberty and the pursuit of Happiness. — That to secure these rights, Governments are instituted among Men, deriving their just powers from the consent of the governed, — That whenever any Form of Government becomes destructive of these ends, it is the Right of the People to alter or to abolish it, and to institute new Government, laying its foundation on such principles and organizing its powers in such form, as to them shall seem most likely to effect their Safety and Happiness. Prudence, indeed, will dictate that Governments long established should not be changed for light and transient causes; and accordingly all experience hath shewn that mankind are more disposed to suffer, while evils are sufferable than to right themselves by abolishing the forms to which they are accustomed. But when a long train of abuses and usurpations, pursuing invariably the same Object evinces a design to reduce them under absolute Despotism, it is their right, it is their duty, to throw off such Government, and to provide new Guards for their future security. — Such has been the patient sufferance of these Colonies; and such is now the necessity which constrains them to alter their former Systems of Government. The history of the present King of Great Britain is a history of repeated injuries and usurpations, all having in direct object the establishment of an absolute Tyranny over these States. To prove this, let Facts be submitted to a candid world.

He has refused his Assent to Laws, the most wholesome and necessary for the public good.

He has forbidden his Governors to pass Laws of immediate and pressing importance, unless suspended in their operation till his Assent should be obtained; and when so suspended, he has utterly neglected to attend to them.

He has refused to pass other Laws for the accommodation of large districts of people, unless those people would relinquish the right of Representation in the Legislature, a right inestimable to them and formidable to tyrants only.

He has called together legislative bodies at places unusual, uncomfortable, and distant from the depository of their Public Records, for the sole purpose of fatiguing them into compliance with his measures.

He has dissolved Representative Houses repeatedly, for opposing with manly firmness his invasions on the rights of the people.

He has refused for a long time, after such dissolutions, to cause others to be elected, whereby the Legislative Powers, incapable of Annihilation, have returned to the People at large for their exercise; the State remaining in the mean time exposed to all the dangers of invasion from without, and convulsions within.

He has endeavoured to prevent the population of these States; for that purpose obstructing the Laws for Naturalization of Foreigners; refusing to pass others to encourage their migrations hither, and raising the conditions of new Appropriations of Lands.

He has obstructed the Administration of Justice by refusing his Assent to Laws for establishing Judiciary Powers.

He has made Judges dependent on his Will alone for the tenure of their offices, and the amount and payment of their salaries.

He has erected a multitude of New Offices, and sent hither swarms of Officers to harass our people and eat out their substance.

He has kept among us, in times of peace, Standing Armies without the Consent of our legislatures.

He has affected to render the Military independent of and superior to the Civil Power.

He has combined with others to subject us to a jurisdiction foreign to our constitution, and unacknowledged by our laws; giving his Assent to their Acts of pretended Legislation:

For quartering large bodies of armed troops among us:

For protecting them, by a mock Trial from punishment for any Murders which they should commit on the Inhabitants of these States:

For cutting off our Trade with all parts of the world:

For imposing Taxes on us without our Consent:

For depriving us in many cases, of the benefit of Trial by Jury:

For transporting us beyond Seas to be tried for pretended offences:

For abolishing the free System of English Laws in a neighbouring Province, establishing therein an Arbitrary government, and enlarging its Boundaries so as to render it at once an example and fit instrument for introducing the same absolute rule into these Colonies

For taking away our Charters, abolishing our most valuable Laws and altering fundamentally the Forms of our Governments:

For suspending our own Legislatures, and declaring themselves invested with power to legislate for us in all cases whatsoever.

He has abdicated Government here, by declaring us out of his Protection and waging War against us.

He has plundered our seas, ravaged our coasts, burnt our towns, and destroyed the lives of our people.

He is at this time transporting large Armies of foreign Mercenaries to compleat the works of death, desolation, and tyranny, already begun with circumstances of Cruelty & Perfidy scarcely paralleled in the most barbarous ages, and totally unworthy the Head of a civilized nation.

He has constrained our fellow Citizens taken Captive on the high Seas to bear Arms against their Country, to become the executioners of their friends and Brethren, or to fall themselves by their Hands.

He has excited domestic insurrections amongst us, and has endeavoured to bring on the inhabitants of our frontiers, the merciless Indian Savages whose known rule of warfare, is an undistinguished destruction of all ages, sexes and conditions.

In every stage of these Oppressions We have Petitioned for Redress in the most humble terms: Our repeated Petitions have been answered only by repeated injury. A Prince, whose character is thus marked by every act which may define a Tyrant, is unfit to be the ruler of a free people.

Nor have We been wanting in attentions to our British brethren. We have warned them from time to time of attempts by their legislature to extend an unwarrantable jurisdiction over us. We have reminded them of the circumstances of our emigration and settlement here. We have appealed to their native justice and magnanimity, and we have conjured them by the ties of our common kindred to disavow these usurpations, which would inevitably interrupt our connections and correspondence. They too have been deaf to the voice of justice and of consanguinity. We must, therefore, acquiesce in the necessity, which denounces our Separation, and hold them, as we hold the rest of mankind, Enemies in War, in Peace Friends.

We, therefore, the Representatives of the united States of America, in General Congress, Assembled, appealing to the Supreme Judge of the world for the rectitude of our intentions, do, in the Name, and by Authority of the good People of these Colonies, solemnly publish and declare, That these united Colonies are, and of Right ought to be Free and Independent States, that they are Absolved from all Allegiance to the British Crown, and that all political connection between them and the State of Great Britain, is and ought to be totally dissolved; and that as Free and Independent States, they have full Power to levy War, conclude Peace, contract Alliances, establish Commerce, and to do all

204 The Bill of Rights 4 Dummmies!

other Acts and Things which Independent States may of right do. — And for the support of this Declaration, with a firm reliance on the protection of Divine Providence, we mutually pledge to each other our Lives, our Fortunes, and our sacred Honor.

— John Hancock

New Hampshire: Josiah Bartlett, William Whipple, Matthew Thornton

Massachusetts: John Hancock, Samuel Adams, John Adams, Robert Treat Paine, Elbridge Gerry

Rhode Island: Stephen Hopkins, William Ellery

Connecticut: Roger Sherman, Samuel Huntington, William Williams, Oliver Wolcott

New York: William Floyd, Philip Livingston, Francis Lewis, Lewis Morris

New Jersey: Richard Stockton, John Witherspoon, Francis Hopkinson, John Hart, Abraham Clark

Pennsylvania: Robert Morris, Benjamin Rush, Benjamin Franklin, John Morton, George Clymer, James Smith, George Taylor, James Wilson, George Ross

Delaware: Caesar Rodney, George Read, Thomas McKean

Maryland: Samuel Chase, William Paca, Thomas Stone, Charles Carroll of Carrollton

Virginia: George Wythe, Richard Henry Lee, Thomas Jefferson, Benjamin Harrison, Thomas Nelson, Jr., Francis Lightfoot Lee, Carter Braxton

North Carolina: William Hooper, Joseph Hewes, John Penn

South Carolina: Edward Rutledge, Thomas Heyward, Jr., Thomas Lynch, Jr., Arthur Middleton

Georgia: Button Gwinnett, Lyman Hall, George Walton

Appendix D: The Articles of Confederation

The Articles of Confederation was an agreement among the 13 founding states that established the United States of America as a confederation of sovereign states and served as its first constitution. The full text of the Articles of Confederation with proper explanations is displayed in this Appendix.

-

The Articles of Confederation

Agreed to by Congress November 15, 1777; ratified and in force, March 1, 1781.

Preamble:
To all to whom these Presents shall come, we the undersigned Delegates of the States affixed to our Names send greeting.

Articles of Confederation and perpetual Union between the States of New Hampshire, Massachusetts bay, Rhode Island and Providence Plantations, Connecticut, New York, New Jersey, Pennsylvania, Delaware, Maryland, Virginia, North Carolina, South Carolina and Georgia.

Article I. The Stile of this Confederacy shall be "The United States of America."

Article II. Each state retains its sovereignty, freedom, and independence, and every power, jurisdiction, and right, which is not by this Confederation expressly delegated to the United States, in Congress assembled.

Article III. The said States hereby severally enter into a firm league of friendship with each other, for their common defense, the security of their liberties, and their mutual and general welfare, binding themselves to assist each other, against all force offered to, or attacks made upon them, or any of them, on account of religion, sovereignty, trade, or any other pretense whatever.

Article IV. The better to secure and perpetuate mutual friendship and intercourse among the people of the different States in this Union, the free inhabitants of each of these States, paupers, vagabonds, and fugitives from justice excepted, shall be entitled to all privileges and immunities of free citizens in the several States; and the people of each State shall free ingress and regress to and from any other State, and shall enjoy therein all the privileges of trade and commerce, subject to the same duties, impositions, and restrictions as the inhabitants thereof respectively, provided that such restrictions shall not extend so far as to prevent the removal of property imported into any State, to any other State, of which the owner is an inhabitant; provided also that no imposition, duties or restriction shall be laid by any State, on the property of the United States, or either of them.

If any person guilty of, or charged with, treason, felony, or other high misdemeanor in any State, shall flee from justice, and be found in any of the United States, he shall, upon demand of the Governor or executive power of the State from which he fled, be delivered up and removed to the State having jurisdiction of his offense.

Full faith and credit shall be given in each of these States to the records, acts, and judicial proceedings of the courts and magistrates of every other State.

Article V. For the most convenient management of the general interests of the United States, delegates shall be annually appointed in such manner as the legislatures of each State shall direct, to meet in Congress on the first Monday in November, in every year, with a power reserved to each State to recall its delegates, or any of them, at any time within the year, and to send others in their stead for the remainder of the year.

No State shall be represented in Congress by less than two, nor more than seven members; and no person shall be capable of being a delegate for more than three years in any term of six years; nor shall any person, being a delegate, be capable of holding any office under the United States, for which he, or another for his benefit, receives any salary, fees or emolument of any kind.

Each State shall maintain its own delegates in a meeting of the States, and while they act as members of the committee of the States.

In determining questions in the United States in Congress assembled, each State shall have one vote.

Freedom of speech and debate in Congress shall not be impeached or questioned in any court or place out of Congress, and the members of Congress shall be protected in their persons from arrests or imprisonments, during the time of their going to and from, and attendance on Congress, except for treason, felony, or breach of the peace.

Article VI. No State, without the consent of the United States in Congress assembled, shall send any embassy to, or receive any embassy from, or enter into any conference, agreement, alliance or treaty with any King, Prince or State; nor shall any person holding any office of profit or trust under the United States, or any of them, accept any present, emolument, office or title of any kind whatever from any King, Prince or foreign State; nor shall the United States in Congress assembled, or any of them, grant any title of nobility.

No two or more States shall enter into any treaty, confederation or alliance whatever between them, without the consent of the United States in Congress assembled, specifying accurately the purposes for which the same is to be entered into, and how long it shall continue.

No State shall lay any imposts or duties, which may interfere with any stipulations in treaties, entered into by the United States in Congress assembled, with any King, Prince or State, in pursuance of any treaties already proposed by Congress, to the courts of France and Spain.

No vessel of war shall be kept up in time of peace by any State, except such number only, as shall be deemed necessary by the United States in Congress assembled, for the defense of such State, or its trade; nor shall any body of forces be kept up by any State in time of peace, except such number only, as in the judgement of the United States in Congress assembled, shall be deemed requisite to garrison the forts necessary for the defense of such State; but every State shall always keep up a well-regulated and disciplined militia, sufficiently armed and accoutered, and shall provide and constantly have ready for use, in public stores, a due number of filed pieces and tents, and a proper quantity of arms, ammunition and camp equipage.

No State shall engage in any war without the consent of the United States in Congress assembled, unless such State be actually invaded by enemies, or shall have received certain advice of a resolution being formed by some nation of Indians to invade such State, and the danger is so imminent as not to admit of a delay till the United States in Congress assembled can be consulted; nor shall any State grant commissions to any ships or vessels of war, nor letters of marque or reprisal, except it be after a declaration of war by the United States in Congress assembled, and then only against the Kingdom or State and the subjects thereof, against which war has been so declared, and under such regulations as shall be established by the United States in Congress assembled, unless such State be infested by pirates, in which case vessels of war may be fitted out for that occasion, and kept so long as the danger shall continue, or until the United States in Congress assembled shall determine otherwise.

Article VII. When land forces are raised by any State for the common defense, all officers of or under the rank of colonel, shall be appointed by the legislature of each State respectively, by whom such forces shall be raised, or in such manner as such State shall direct, and all vacancies shall be filled up by the State which first made the appointment.

Article VIII. All charges of war, and all other expenses that shall be incurred for the common defense or general welfare, and allowed by the United States in Congress assembled, shall be defrayed out of a common treasury, which shall be supplied by the several States in proportion to the value of all land within each State, granted or surveyed for any person, as such land and the buildings and improvements thereon shall be estimated according to such mode as the United States in Congress assembled, shall from time to time direct and appoint.
The taxes for paying that proportion shall be laid and levied by the authority and direction of the legislatures of the several States within the time agreed upon by the United States in Congress assembled.

Article IX. The United States in Congress assembled, shall have the sole and exclusive right and power of determining on peace and war, except in the cases mentioned in the sixth article — of sending and receiving ambassadors — entering into treaties and alliances, provided that no treaty of commerce shall be made whereby the legislative power of the respective States shall be restrained from imposing such imposts and duties on foreigners, as their own people are subjected to, or from prohibiting the exportation or importation of any species of goods or commodities whatsoever — of establishing rules for deciding in all cases, what captures on land or water shall be legal, and in what manner prizes taken by land or naval forces in the service of the United States shall be divided or appropriated — of granting letters of marque and reprisal in times of peace — appointing courts for the trial of piracies and felonies committed on the high seas and establishing courts for receiving and determining finally appeals in all cases of captures, provided that no member of Congress shall be appointed a judge of any of the said courts.

The United States in Congress assembled shall also be the last resort on appeal in all disputes and differences now subsisting or that hereafter may arise between two or more States concerning boundary, jurisdiction or any other causes whatever; which authority shall always be exercised in the manner following. Whenever the legislative or executive authority or lawful agent of any State in controversy with another shall present a petition to Congress stating the matter in question and praying for a hearing, notice thereof shall be given by order of Congress to the legislative or executive authority of the other State in controversy, and a day assigned for the appearance of the parties by their lawful agents, who shall then be directed to appoint by joint consent, commissioners or judges to constitute a court for hearing and determining the matter in question: but if they cannot agree, Congress shall name three persons out of each of the United States, and from the list of such persons each party shall alternately strike out one, the petitioners beginning, until the number shall be reduced to thirteen; and from that number not less than seven, nor more than nine names as Congress shall direct, shall in the presence of Congress be drawn out by lot, and the persons whose names shall be so drawn or any five of them, shall be commissioners or judges, to hear and finally determine the controversy, so always as a major part of the judges who shall hear the cause shall agree in the determination: and if either party shall neglect to attend at the day appointed, without showing reasons, which Congress shall judge sufficient, or being present shall refuse to strike, the Congress shall proceed to nominate three persons out of each State, and the secretary of Congress shall strike in behalf of such party absent or refusing; and the judgment and sentence of the court to be appointed, in the manner before prescribed, shall be final and conclusive; and if any of the parties shall refuse to submit to the authority of such court, or to appear or defend their claim or cause, the court shall nevertheless proceed to pronounce sentence, or judgment, which shall in like manner be final and decisive, the judgment or sentence and other proceedings being in either case transmitted to Congress, and lodged among the acts of Congress for the security of the parties concerned: provided that every commissioner, before he sits in judgment, shall take an oath to be administered by one of the judges of the supreme or superior court of the State, where the cause shall be tried, 'well and truly to hear and determine the matter in question, according to the best of his judgment, without favor, affection or hope of reward': provided also, that no State shall be deprived of territory for the benefit of the United States.

All controversies concerning the private right of soil claimed under different grants of two or more States, whose jurisdictions as they may respect such lands, and the States which passed such grants are adjusted, the said grants or either of them being at the same time claimed to have originated antecedent to such settlement of jurisdiction, shall on the petition of either party to the Congress of the United States, be finally determined as near as may be in the same manner as is before prescribed for deciding disputes respecting territorial jurisdiction between different States.

The United States in Congress assembled shall also have the sole and exclusive right and power of regulating the alloy and value of coin struck by their own authority, or by that of the respective States — fixing the standards of weights and measures throughout the United States — regulating the trade and managing all affairs with the Indians, not members of any of the States, provided that the legislative right of any State within its own limits be not infringed or violated — establishing or regulating post offices from one State to another, throughout all the United States, and exacting such postage on the papers passing through the same as may be requisite to defray the expenses of the said office — appointing all officers of the land forces, in the service of the United States, excepting regimental officers — appointing all the officers of the naval forces, and commissioning all officers whatever in the service of the United States — making rules for the government and regulation of the said land and naval forces, and directing their operations.

The United States in Congress assembled shall have authority to appoint a committee, to sit in the recess of Congress, to be denominated 'A Committee of the States', and to consist of one delegate from each State; and to appoint such other committees and civil officers as may be necessary for managing the general affairs of the United States under their direction — to appoint one of their members to preside, provided that no person be allowed to serve in the office of president more than one year in any term of three years; to ascertain the necessary sums of money to be raised for the service of the United States, and to appropriate and apply the same for defraying the public expenses — to borrow money, or emit bills on the credit of the United States, transmitting every half-year to the respective States an account of the sums of money so borrowed or emitted — to build and equip a navy — to agree upon the number of land forces, and to make requisitions from each State for its quota, in proportion to the number of white inhabitants in such State; which requisition shall be binding, and thereupon the legislature of each State shall appoint the regimental officers, raise the men and cloath, arm and equip them in a solid-like manner, at the expense of the United States; and the officers and men so cloathed, armed and equipped shall march to the place appointed, and within the time agreed on by the United States in Congress assembled. But if the United States in Congress assembled shall, on consideration of circumstances judge proper that any State should not raise men, or should raise a smaller number of men than the quota thereof, such extra number shall be raised, officered, cloathed, armed and equipped in the same manner as the quota of each State, unless the legislature of such State shall judge that such extra number cannot be safely spread out in the same, in which case they shall raise, officer, cloath, arm and equip as many of such extra number as they judge can be safely spared. And the officers and men so cloathed, armed, and equipped, shall march to the place appointed, and within the time agreed on by the United States in Congress assembled.

The United States in Congress assembled shall never engage in a war, nor grant letters of marque or reprisal in time of peace, nor enter into any treaties or alliances, nor coin money, nor regulate the value thereof, nor ascertain the sums and expenses necessary for the defense and welfare of the United States, or any of them, nor emit bills, nor borrow money on the credit of the United States, nor appropriate money, nor agree upon the number of vessels of war, to be built or purchased, or the number of land or sea forces to be raised, nor appoint a commander in chief of the army or navy, unless nine States assent to the same: nor shall a question on any other point, except for adjourning from day to day be determined, unless by the votes of the majority of the United States in Congress assembled.

The Congress of the United States shall have power to adjourn to any time within the year, and to any place within the United States, so that no period of adjournment be for a longer duration than the space of six months, and shall publish the journal of their proceedings monthly, except such parts thereof relating to treaties, alliances or military operations, as in their judgement require secrecy; and the yeas and nays of the delegates of each State on any question shall be entered on the journal, when it is desired by any delegates of a State, or any of them, at his or their request shall be furnished with a transcript of the said journal, except such parts as are above excepted, to lay before the legislatures of the several States.

Article X. The Committee of the States, or any nine of them, shall be authorized to execute, in the recess of Congress, such of the powers of Congress as the United States in Congress assembled, by the consent of the nine States, shall from time to time think expedient to vest them with; provided that no power be delegated to the said Committee, for the exercise of which, by the Articles of Confederation, the voice of nine States in the Congress of the United States assembled be requisite.

Article XI. Canada acceding to this confederation, and adjoining in the measures of the United States, shall be admitted into, and entitled to all the advantages of this Union; but no other colony shall be admitted into the same, unless such admission be agreed to by nine States.

Article XII. All bills of credit emitted, monies borrowed, and debts contracted by, or under the authority of Congress, before the assembling of the United States, in pursuance of the present confederation, shall be deemed and considered as a charge against the United States, for payment and satisfaction whereof the said United States, and the public faith are hereby solemnly pledged.

Article XIII. Every State shall abide by the determination of the United States in Congress assembled, on all questions which by this confederation are submitted to them. And the Articles of this Confederation shall be inviolably observed by every State, and the Union shall be perpetual; nor shall any alteration at any time hereafter be made in any of them; unless such alteration be agreed to in a Congress of the United States, and be afterwards confirmed by the legislatures of every State.

And Whereas it hath pleased the Great Governor of the World to incline the hearts of the legislatures we respectively represent in Congress, to approve of, and to authorize us to ratify the said Articles of Confederation and perpetual Union. Know Ye that we the undersigned delegates, by virtue of the power and authority to us given for that purpose, do by these presents, in the name and in behalf of our respective constituents, fully and entirely ratify and confirm each and every of the said Articles of Confederation and perpetual Union, and all and singular the matters and things therein contained: And we do further solemnly plight and engage the faith of our respective constituents, that they shall abide by the determinations of the United States in Congress assembled, on all questions, which by the said Confederation are submitted to them. And that the Articles thereof shall be inviolably observed by the States we respectively represent, and that the Union shall be perpetual.

In Witness whereof we have hereunto set our hands in Congress. Done at Philadelphia in the State of Pennsylvania the ninth day of July in the Year of our Lord One Thousand Seven Hundred and Seventy-Eight, and in the Third Year of the independence of America.

On the part and behalf of the State of New Hampshire:
Josiah Bartlett, John Wentworth Junior. August 8th 1778

On the part and behalf of The State of Massachusetts Bay:
John Hancock, Samuel Adams, Elbridge Gerry, Francis Dana, James Lovell, Samuel Holten

On the part and behalf of the State of Rhode Island and Providence Plantations:
William Ellery, Henry Marchant, John Collins

On the part and behalf of the State of Connecticut:
Roger Sherman, Samuel Huntington, Oliver Wolcott, Titus Hosmer, Andrew Adams

On the part and behalf of the State of New York:
James Duane, Francis Lewis, William Duer, Gouv Morris

On the part and behalf of the State of New Jersey: November 26, 1778.
John Witherspoon, Nathan Scudder

On the part and behalf of the State of Pennsylvania:
Robert Morris, Daniel Roberdeau, John Bayard Smith, William Clingan,
Joseph Reed 22nd July 1778

On the part and behalf of the State of Delaware:
Thomas Mckean February 12, 1779, John Dickinson May 5th 1779,
Nicholas Van Dyke

On the part and behalf of the State of Maryland:
John Hanson March 1 1781, Daniel Carroll

On the part and behalf of the State of Virginia:
Richard Henry Lee, John Banister, Thomas Adams, John Harvie,
Francis Lightfoot Lee

On the part and behalf of the State of No Carolina:
John Penn July 21st 1778, Cornelius Harnett, John Williams

On the part and behalf of the State of South Carolina:
Henry Laurens, William Henry Drayton, John Mathews, Richard Hutson,
Thomas Heyward Junior

On the part and behalf of the State of Georgia:
John Walton 24th July 1778, Edward Telfair, Edward Langworthy

Appendix E   The Constitution of the United States of America

----
-

The Constitution of the United States: A Transcription

Note: The following text is a transcription of the Constitution in its original form. Items that are hyperlinked have since been amended or superseded.

We the People of the United States, in Order to form a more perfect Union, establish Justice, insure domestic Tranquility, provide for the common defence, promote the general Welfare, and secure the Blessings of Liberty to ourselves and our Posterity, do ordain and establish this Constitution for the United States of America.

Article. I.

Section. 1.
All legislative Powers herein granted shall be vested in a Congress of the United States, which shall consist of a Senate and House of Representatives.

Section. 2.
The House of Representatives shall be composed of Members chosen every second Year by the People of the several States, and the Electors in each State shall have the Qualifications requisite for Electors of the most numerous Branch of the State Legislature.

No Person shall be a Representative who shall not have attained to the Age of twenty five Years, and been seven Years a Citizen of the United States, and who shall not, when elected, be an Inhabitant of that State in which he shall be chosen.

Representatives and direct Taxes shall be apportioned among the several States which may be included within this Union, according to their respective Numbers, which shall be determined by adding to the whole Number of free Persons, including those bound to Service for a Term of Years, and excluding Indians not taxed, three fifths of all other Persons. The actual Enumeration shall be made within three Years after the first Meeting of the Congress of the United States, and within every subsequent Term of ten Years, in such Manner as they shall by Law direct. The Number of Representatives shall not exceed one for every thirty Thousand, but each State shall have at Least one Representative; and until such enumeration shall be made, the State of New Hampshire shall be entitled to chuse three, Massachusetts eight, Rhode-Island and Providence Plantations one, Connecticut five, New-York six, New Jersey four, Pennsylvania eight, Delaware one, Maryland six, Virginia ten, North Carolina five, South Carolina five, and Georgia three.

When vacancies happen in the Representation from any State, the Executive Authority thereof shall issue Writs of Election to fill such Vacancies.

The House of Representatives shall chuse their Speaker and other Officers; and shall have the sole Power of Impeachment.

Section. 3.
The Senate of the United States shall be composed of two Senators from each State, chosen by the Legislature thereof for six Years; and each Senator shall have one Vote.

Immediately after they shall be assembled in Consequence of the first Election, they shall be divided as equally as may be into three Classes. The Seats of the Senators of the first Class shall be vacated at the Expiration of the second Year, of the second Class at the Expiration of the fourth Year, and of the third Class at the Expiration of the sixth Year, so that one third may be chosen every second Year; and if Vacancies happen by Resignation, or otherwise, during the Recess of the Legislature of any State, the Executive thereof may make temporary Appointments until the next Meeting of the Legislature, which shall then fill such Vacancies.

No Person shall be a Senator who shall not have attained to the Age of thirty Years, and been nine Years a Citizen of the United States, and who shall not, when elected, be an Inhabitant of that State for which he shall be chosen.

The Vice President of the United States shall be President of the Senate, but shall have no Vote, unless they be equally divided.

The Senate shall chuse their other Officers, and also a President pro tempore, in the Absence of the Vice President, or when he shall exercise the Office of President of the United States.

The Senate shall have the sole Power to try all Impeachments. When sitting for that Purpose, they shall be on Oath or Affirmation. When the President of the United States is tried, the Chief Justice shall preside: And no Person shall be convicted without the Concurrence of two thirds of the Members present.

Judgment in Cases of Impeachment shall not extend further than to removal from Office, and disqualification to hold and enjoy any Office of honor, Trust or Profit under the United States: but the Party convicted shall nevertheless be liable and subject to Indictment, Trial, Judgment and Punishment, according to Law.

Section. 4.
The Times, Places and Manner of holding Elections for Senators and Representatives, shall be prescribed in each State by the Legislature thereof; but the Congress may at any time by Law make or alter such Regulations, except as to the Places of chusing Senators.

The Congress shall assemble at least once in every Year, and such Meeting shall be on the first Monday in December, unless they shall by Law appoint a different Day.

Section. 5.
Each House shall be the Judge of the Elections, Returns and Qualifications of its own Members, and a Majority of each shall constitute a Quorum to do Business; but a smaller Number may adjourn from day to day, and may be authorized to compel the Attendance of absent Members, in such Manner, and under such Penalties as each House may provide.

Each House may determine the Rules of its Proceedings, punish its Members for disorderly Behaviour, and, with the Concurrence of two thirds, expel a Member.

Each House shall keep a Journal of its Proceedings, and from time to time publish the same, excepting such Parts as may in their Judgment require Secrecy; and the Yeas and Nays of the Members of either House on any question shall, at the Desire of one fifth of those Present, be entered on the Journal.

Neither House, during the Session of Congress, shall, without the Consent of the other, adjourn for more than three days, nor to any other Place than that in which the two Houses shall be sitting.

Section. 6.
The Senators and Representatives shall receive a Compensation for their Services, to be ascertained by Law, and paid out of the Treasury of the United States. They shall in all Cases, except Treason, Felony and Breach of the Peace, be privileged from Arrest during their Attendance at the Session of their respective Houses, and in going to and returning from the same; and for any Speech or Debate in either House, they shall not be questioned in any other Place.

No Senator or Representative shall, during the Time for which he was elected, be appointed to any civil Office under the Authority of the United States, which shall have been created, or the Emoluments whereof shall have been encreased during such time; and no Person holding any Office under the United States, shall be a Member of either House during his Continuance in Office.

Section. 7.
All Bills for raising Revenue shall originate in the House of Representatives; but the Senate may propose or concur with Amendments as on other Bills.

Every Bill which shall have passed the House of Representatives and the Senate, shall, before it become a Law, be presented to the President of the United States: If he approve he shall sign it, but if not he shall return it, with his Objections to that House in which it shall have originated, who shall enter the Objections at large on their Journal, and proceed to reconsider it. If after such Reconsideration two thirds of that House shall agree to pass the Bill, it shall be sent, together with the Objections, to the other House, by which it shall likewise be reconsidered, and if approved by two thirds of that House, it shall become a Law. But in all such Cases the Votes of both Houses shall be determined by yeas and Nays, and the Names of the Persons voting for and against the Bill shall be entered on the Journal of each House respectively. If any Bill shall not be returned by the President within ten Days (Sundays excepted) after it shall have been presented to him, the Same shall be a Law, in like Manner as if he had signed it, unless the Congress by their Adjournment prevent its Return, in which Case it shall not be a Law.

Every Order, Resolution, or Vote to which the Concurrence of the Senate and House of Representatives may be necessary (except on a question of Adjournment) shall be presented to the President of the United States; and before the Same shall take Effect, shall be approved by him, or being disapproved by him, shall be repassed by two thirds of the Senate and House of Representatives, according to the Rules and Limitations prescribed in the Case of a Bill.

Section. 8.

The Congress shall have Power To lay and collect Taxes, Duties, Imposts and Excises, to pay the Debts and provide for the common Defence and general Welfare of the United States; but all Duties, Imposts and Excises shall be uniform throughout the United States;

*To borrow Money on the credit of the United States;

*To regulate Commerce with foreign Nations, and among the several States, and with the Indian Tribes;

*To establish an uniform Rule of Naturalization, and uniform Laws on the subject of Bankruptcies throughout the United States;

*To coin Money, regulate the Value thereof, and of foreign Coin, and fix the Standard of Weights and Measures;

*To provide for the Punishment of counterfeiting the Securities and current Coin of the United States;

*To establish Post Offices and post Roads;

*To promote the Progress of Science and useful Arts, by securing for limited Times to Authors and Inventors the exclusive Right to their respective Writings and Discoveries;

*To constitute Tribunals inferior to the supreme Court;

*To define and punish Piracies and Felonies committed on the high Seas, and Offences against the Law of Nations;

*To declare War, grant Letters of Marque and Reprisal, and make Rules concerning Captures on Land and Water;

*To raise and support Armies, but no Appropriation of Money to that Use shall be for a longer Term than two Years;

*To provide and maintain a Navy;

*To make Rules for the Government and Regulation of the land and naval Forces;

*To provide for calling forth the Militia to execute the Laws of the Union, suppress Insurrections and repel Invasions;

*To provide for organizing, arming, and disciplining, the Militia, and for governing such Part of them as may be employed in the Service of the United States, reserving to the States respectively, the Appointment of the Officers, and the Authority of training the Militia according to the discipline prescribed by Congress;

*To exercise exclusive Legislation in all Cases whatsoever, over such District (not exceeding ten Miles square) as may, by Cession of particular States, and the Acceptance of Congress, become the Seat of the Government of the United States, and to exercise like Authority over all Places purchased by the Consent of the Legislature of the State in which the Same shall be, for the Erection of Forts, Magazines, Arsenals, dock-Yards, and other needful Buildings;--And

*To make all Laws which shall be necessary and proper for carrying into Execution the foregoing Powers, and all other Powers vested by this Constitution in the Government of the United States, or in any Department or Officer thereof.

Section. 9.

The Migration or Importation of such Persons as any of the States now existing shall think proper to admit, shall not be prohibited by the Congress prior to the Year one thousand eight hundred and eight, but a Tax or duty may be imposed on such Importation, not exceeding ten dollars for each Person.

The Privilege of the Writ of Habeas Corpus shall not be suspended, unless when in Cases of Rebellion or Invasion the public Safety may require it.

No Bill of Attainder or ex post facto Law shall be passed.

No Capitation, or other direct, Tax shall be laid, unless in Proportion to the Census or enumeration herein before directed to be taken.

No Tax or Duty shall be laid on Articles exported from any State.

No Preference shall be given by any Regulation of Commerce or Revenue to the Ports of one State over those of another; nor shall Vessels bound to, or from, one State, be obliged to enter, clear, or pay Duties in another.

No Money shall be drawn from the Treasury, but in Consequence of Appropriations made by Law; and a regular Statement and Account of the Receipts and Expenditures of all public Money shall be published from time to time.

No Title of Nobility shall be granted by the United States: And no Person holding any Office of Profit or Trust under them, shall, without the Consent of the Congress, accept of any present, Emolument, Office, or Title, of any kind whatever, from any King, Prince, or foreign State.

Section. 10.
No State shall enter into any Treaty, Alliance, or Confederation; grant Letters of Marque and Reprisal; coin Money; emit Bills of Credit; make any Thing but gold and silver Coin a Tender in Payment of Debts; pass any Bill of Attainder, ex post facto Law, or Law impairing the Obligation of Contracts, or grant any Title of Nobility.

No State shall, without the Consent of the Congress, lay any Imposts or Duties on Imports or Exports, except what may be absolutely necessary for executing it's inspection Laws: and the net Produce of all Duties and Imposts, laid by any State on Imports or Exports, shall be for the Use of the Treasury of the United States; and all such Laws shall be subject to the Revision and Controul of the Congress.

No State shall, without the Consent of Congress, lay any Duty of Tonnage, keep Troops, or Ships of War in time of Peace, enter into any Agreement or Compact with another State, or with a foreign Power, or engage in War, unless actually invaded, or in such imminent Danger as will not admit of delay.

Article. II.
Section. 1.
The executive Power shall be vested in a President of the United States of America. He shall hold his Office during the Term of four Years, and, together with the Vice President, chosen for the same Term, be elected, as follows:

Each State shall appoint, in such Manner as the Legislature thereof may direct, a Number of Electors, equal to the whole Number of Senators and Representatives to which the State may be entitled in the Congress: but no Senator or Representative, or Person holding an Office of Trust or Profit under the United States, shall be appointed an Elector.

The Electors shall meet in their respective States, and vote by Ballot for two Persons, of whom one at least shall not be an Inhabitant of the same State with themselves. And they shall make a List of all the Persons voted for, and of the Number of Votes for each; which List they shall sign and certify, and transmit sealed to the Seat of the Government of the United States, directed to the President of the Senate. The President of the Senate shall, in the Presence of the Senate and House of Representatives, open all the Certificates, and the Votes shall then be counted. The Person having the greatest Number of Votes shall be the President, if such Number be a Majority of the whole Number of Electors appointed; and if there be more than one who have such Majority, and have an equal Number of Votes, then the House of Representatives shall immediately chuse by Ballot one of them for President; and if no Person have a Majority, then from the five highest on the List the said House shall in like Manner chuse the President. But in chusing the President, the Votes shall be taken by States, the Representation from each State having one Vote; A quorum for this purpose shall consist of a Member or Members from two thirds of the States, and a Majority of all the States shall be necessary to a Choice. In every Case, after the Choice of the President, the Person having the greatest Number of Votes of the Electors shall be the Vice President. But if there should remain two or more who have equal Votes, the Senate shall chuse from them by Ballot the Vice President.

The Congress may determine the Time of chusing the Electors, and the Day on which they shall give their Votes; which Day shall be the same throughout the United States.

No Person except a natural born Citizen, or a Citizen of the United States, at the time of the Adoption of this Constitution, shall be eligible to the Office of President; neither shall any Person be eligible to that Office who shall not have attained to the Age of thirty five Years, and been fourteen Years a Resident within the United States.

In Case of the Removal of the President from Office, or of his Death, Resignation, or Inability to discharge the Powers and Duties of the said Office, the Same shall devolve on the Vice President, and the Congress may by Law provide for the Case of Removal, Death, Resignation or Inability, both of the President and Vice President, declaring what Officer shall then act as President, and such Officer shall act accordingly, until the Disability be removed, or a President shall be elected.

The President shall, at stated Times, receive for his Services, a Compensation, which shall neither be increased nor diminished during the Period for which he shall have been elected, and he shall not receive within that Period any other Emolument from the United States, or any of them.

Before he enter on the Execution of his Office, he shall take the following Oath or Affirmation:--"I do solemnly swear (or affirm) that I will faithfully execute the Office of President of the United States, and will to the best of my Ability, preserve, protect and defend the Constitution of the United States."

Section. 2.
The President shall be Commander in Chief of the Army and Navy of the United States, and of the Militia of the several States, when called into the actual Service of the United States; he may require the Opinion, in writing, of the principal Officer in each of the executive Departments, upon any Subject relating to the Duties of their respective Offices, and he shall have Power to grant Reprieves and Pardons for Offences against the United States, except in Cases of Impeachment.

He shall have Power, by and with the Advice and Consent of the Senate, to make Treaties, provided two thirds of the Senators present concur; and he shall nominate, and by and with the Advice and Consent of the Senate, shall appoint Ambassadors, other public Ministers and Consuls, Judges of the supreme Court, and all other Officers of the United States, whose Appointments are not herein otherwise provided for, and which shall be established by Law: but the Congress may by Law vest the Appointment of such inferior Officers, as they think proper, in the President alone, in the Courts of Law, or in the Heads of Departments.

The President shall have Power to fill up all Vacancies that may happen during the Recess of the Senate, by granting Commissions which shall expire at the End of their next Session.

Section. 3.

He shall from time to time give to the Congress Information of the State of the Union, and recommend to their Consideration such Measures as he shall judge necessary and expedient; he may, on extraordinary Occasions, convene both Houses, or either of them, and in Case of Disagreement between them, with Respect to the Time of Adjournment, he may adjourn them to such Time as he shall think proper; he shall receive Ambassadors and other public Ministers; he shall take Care that the Laws be faithfully executed, and shall Commission all the Officers of the United States.

Section. 4.

The President, Vice President and all civil Officers of the United States, shall be removed from Office on Impeachment for, and Conviction of, Treason, Bribery, or other high Crimes and Misdemeanors.

Article III.

Section. 1.

The judicial Power of the United States shall be vested in one supreme Court, and in such inferior Courts as the Congress may from time to time ordain and establish. The Judges, both of the supreme and inferior Courts, shall hold their Offices during good Behaviour, and shall, at stated Times, receive for their Services a Compensation, which shall not be diminished during their Continuance in Office.

Section. 2.

The judicial Power shall extend to all Cases, in Law and Equity, arising under this Constitution, the Laws of the United States, and Treaties made, or which shall be made, under their Authority;--to all Cases affecting Ambassadors, other public Ministers and Consuls;--to all Cases of admiralty and maritime Jurisdiction;--to Controversies to which the United States shall be a Party;--to Controversies between two or more States;--between a State and Citizens of another State;--between Citizens of different States;--between Citizens of the same State claiming Lands under Grants of different States, and between a State, or the Citizens thereof, and foreign States, Citizens or Subjects.

In all Cases affecting Ambassadors, other public Ministers and Consuls, and those in which a State shall be Party, the supreme Court shall have original Jurisdiction. In all the other Cases before mentioned, the supreme Court shall have appellate Jurisdiction, both as to Law and Fact, with such Exceptions, and under such Regulations as the Congress shall make.

The Trial of all Crimes, except in Cases of Impeachment, shall be by Jury; and such Trial shall be held in the State where the said Crimes shall have been committed; but when not committed within any State, the Trial shall be at such Place or Places as the Congress may by Law have directed.

Section. 3.

Treason against the United States, shall consist only in levying War against them, or in adhering to their Enemies, giving them Aid and Comfort. No Person shall be convicted of Treason unless on the Testimony of two Witnesses to the same overt Act, or on Confession in open Court.

The Congress shall have Power to declare the Punishment of Treason, but no Attainder of Treason shall work Corruption of Blood, or Forfeiture except during the Life of the Person attainted.

Article. IV.

Section. 1.
Full Faith and Credit shall be given in each State to the public Acts, Records, and judicial Proceedings of every other State. And the Congress may by general Laws prescribe the Manner in which such Acts, Records and Proceedings shall be proved, and the Effect thereof.

Section. 2.
The Citizens of each State shall be entitled to all Privileges and Immunities of Citizens in the several States.

A Person charged in any State with Treason, Felony, or other Crime, who shall flee from Justice, and be found in another State, shall on Demand of the executive Authority of the State from which he fled, be delivered up, to be removed to the State having Jurisdiction of the Crime.

No Person held to Service or Labour in one State, under the Laws thereof, escaping into another, shall, in Consequence of any Law or Regulation therein, be discharged from such Service or Labour, but shall be delivered up on Claim of the Party to whom such Service or Labour may be due.

Section. 3.
New States may be admitted by the Congress into this Union; but no new State shall be formed or erected within the Jurisdiction of any other State; nor any State be formed by the Junction of two or more States, or Parts of States, without the Consent of the Legislatures of the States concerned as well as of the Congress.

The Congress shall have Power to dispose of and make all needful Rules and Regulations respecting the Territory or other Property belonging to the United States; and nothing in this Constitution shall be so construed as to Prejudice any Claims of the United States, or of any particular State.

Section. 4.
The United States shall guarantee to every State in this Union a Republican Form of Government, and shall protect each of them against Invasion; and on Application of the Legislature, or of the Executive (when the Legislature cannot be convened), against domestic Violence.

Article. V.

The Congress, whenever two thirds of both Houses shall deem it necessary, shall propose Amendments to this Constitution, or, on the Application of the Legislatures of two thirds of the several States, shall call a Convention for proposing Amendments, which, in either Case, shall be valid to all Intents and Purposes, as Part of this Constitution, when ratified by the Legislatures of three fourths of the several States, or by Conventions in three fourths thereof, as the one or the other Mode of Ratification may be proposed by the Congress; Provided that no Amendment which may be made prior to the Year One thousand eight hundred and eight shall in any Manner affect the first and fourth Clauses in the Ninth Section of the first Article; and that no State, without its Consent, shall be deprived of its equal Suffrage in the Senate.

Article. VI.

All Debts contracted and Engagements entered into, before the Adoption of this Constitution, shall be as valid against the United States under this Constitution, as under the Confederation.

This Constitution, and the Laws of the United States which shall be made in Pursuance thereof; and all Treaties made, or which shall be made, under the Authority of the United States, shall be the supreme Law of the Land; and the Judges in every State shall be bound thereby, any Thing in the Constitution or Laws of any State to the Contrary notwithstanding.

The Senators and Representatives before mentioned, and the Members of the several State Legislatures, and all executive and judicial Officers, both of the United States and of the several States, shall be bound by Oath or Affirmation, to support this Constitution; but no religious Test shall ever be required as a Qualification to any Office or public Trust under the United States.

Article. VII.

The Ratification of the Conventions of nine States, shall be sufficient for the Establishment of this Constitution between the States so ratifying the Same.

The Word, "the," being interlined between the seventh and eighth Lines of the first Page, the Word "Thirty" being partly written on an Erazure in the fifteenth Line of the first Page, The Words "is tried" being interlined between the thirty second and thirty third Lines of the first Page and the Word "the" being interlined between the forty third and forty fourth Lines of the second Page.
Attest William Jackson Secretary

Done in Convention by the Unanimous Consent of the States present the Seventeenth Day of September in the Year of our Lord one thousand seven hundred and Eighty seven and of the Independence of the United States of America the Twelfth In witness whereof We have hereunto subscribed our Names,

George Washington
President and Deputy from Virginia

Delaware
Geo Read, Gunning Bedford, John Dickinson, Richard Bassett, Jaco Broom

Maryland
James McHenry, Dan of St Thos. Jenifer Daniel Carroll

Virginia
John Blair, James Madison Jr.

North Carolina
William Blount, Richard Dobbs Spaight, Hume Williamson

South Carolina
J. Rutledge, Charles Cotesworth Pinckney, Charles Pinckney, Pierce Butler

224 The Bill of Rights 4 Dummmies!

Georgia
William Few, Abraham Baldwin

New Hampshire
John Langdon, Nicholas Gilman,

Massachusetts
Nathaniel Gorham, Rufus King

Connecticut
William. Samuel Johnson, Roger Sherman

New York
Alexander Hamilton,

New Jersey
William Livingston, David Brearley, William Paterson, Jonathan Dayton

Pennsylvania
Ben Franklin, Thomas Mifflin, Robert. Morris, George. Clymer,
Thomas. FitzSimons, Jared Ingersoll, James Wilson, Gouv Morris

http://www.archives.gov/national-archives-
experience/charters/constitution_transcript.html

Appendix F   The Bill of Rights & Other Constitutional Amendments

The first ten amendments to the U.S. Constitution are known as The Bill of Rights. Freedom of religion, speech, press, assembly, and petition. Right to keep and bear arms in order to maintain a well-regulated militia. A full explanation is displayed in Chapter 14. The full text of the twenty-seven amendments are also contained in this Appendix.

The Bill of Rights: A Transcription

The Preamble to the Bill of Rights

Congress of the United States -- begun and held at the City of New-York, on Wednesday the fourth of March, one thousand seven hundred and eighty nine.

THE Conventions of a number of the States, having at the time of their adopting the Constitution, expressed a desire, in order to prevent misconstruction or abuse of its powers, that further declaratory and restrictive clauses should be added: And as extending the ground of public confidence in the Government, will best ensure the beneficent ends of its institution.

RESOLVED by the Senate and House of Representatives of the United States of America, in Congress assembled, two thirds of both Houses concurring, that the following Articles be proposed to the Legislatures of the several States, as amendments to the Constitution of the United States, all, or any of which Articles, when ratified by three fourths of the said Legislatures, to be valid to all intents and purposes, as part of the said Constitution; viz.

ARTICLES in addition to, and Amendment of the Constitution of the United States of America, proposed by Congress, and ratified by the Legislatures of the several States, pursuant to the fifth Article of the original Constitution.

Note: The following text is a transcription of the first ten amendments to the Constitution in their original form. These amendments were ratified December 15, 1791, and form what is known as the "Bill of Rights."

Amendment I
Congress shall make no law respecting an establishment of religion, or prohibiting the free exercise thereof; or abridging the freedom of speech, or of the press; or the right of the people peaceably to assemble, and to petition the Government for a redress of grievances.

Amendment II

A well regulated Militia, being necessary to the security of a free State, the right of the people to keep and bear Arms, shall not be infringed.

Amendment III
No Soldier shall, in time of peace be quartered in any house, without the consent of the Owner, nor in time of war, but in a manner to be prescribed by law.

Amendment IV
The right of the people to be secure in their persons, houses, papers, and effects, against unreasonable searches and seizures, shall not be violated, and no Warrants shall issue, but upon probable cause, supported by Oath or affirmation, and particularly describing the place to be searched, and the persons or things to be seized. [No fishing expeditions]

Amendment V
No person shall be held to answer for a capital, or otherwise infamous crime, unless on a presentment or indictment of a Grand Jury, except in cases arising in the land or naval forces, or in the Militia, when in actual service in time of War or public danger; nor shall any person be subject for the same offence to be twice put in jeopardy of life or limb; nor shall be compelled in any criminal case to be a witness against himself, nor be deprived of life, liberty, or property, without due process of law; nor shall private property be taken for public use, without just compensation.

Amendment VI
In all criminal prosecutions, the accused shall enjoy the right to a speedy and public trial, by an impartial jury of the State and district wherein the crime shall have been committed, which district shall have been previously ascertained by law, and to be informed of the nature and cause of the accusation; to be confronted with the witnesses against him; to have compulsory process for obtaining witnesses in his favor, and to have the Assistance of Counsel for his defence.

Amendment VII
In Suits at common law, where the value in controversy shall exceed twenty dollars, the right of trial by jury shall be preserved, and no fact tried by a jury, shall be otherwise re-examined in any Court of the United States, than according to the rules of the common law.

Amendment VIII
Excessive bail shall not be required, nor excessive fines imposed, nor cruel and unusual punishments inflicted.

Amendment IX
The enumeration in the Constitution, of certain rights, shall not be construed to deny or disparage others retained by the people.

Amendment X
The powers not delegated to the United States by the Constitution, nor prohibited by it to the States, are reserved to the States respectively, or to the people.

The Constitution: Amendments 11-27

Constitutional Amendments 1-10 make up what is known as The Bill of Rights. Amendments 11-27 are listed below.

AMENDMENT XI
Passed by Congress March 4, 1794. Ratified February 7, 1795.
Note: Article III, section 2, of the Constitution was modified by amendment 11.
The Judicial power of the United States shall not be construed to extend to any suit in law or equity, commenced or prosecuted against one of the United States by Citizens of another State, or by Citizens or Subjects of any Foreign State.

AMENDMENT XII
Passed by Congress December 9, 1803. Ratified June 15, 1804.

Note: A portion of Article II, section 1 of the Constitution was superseded by the 12th amendment.

The Electors shall meet in their respective states and vote by ballot for President and Vice-President, one of whom, at least, shall not be an inhabitant of the same state with themselves; they shall name in their ballots the person voted for as President, and in distinct ballots the person voted for as Vice-President, and they shall make distinct lists of all persons voted for as President, and of all persons voted for as Vice-President, and of the number of votes for each, which lists they shall sign and certify, and transmit sealed to the seat of the government of the United States, directed to the President of the Senate; -- the President of the Senate shall, in the presence of the Senate and House of Representatives, open all the certificates and the votes shall then be counted; -- The person having the greatest number of votes for President, shall be the President, if such number be a majority of the whole number of Electors appointed; and if no person have such majority, then from the persons having the highest numbers not exceeding three on the list of those voted for as President, the House of Representatives shall choose immediately, by ballot, the President. But in choosing the President, the votes shall be taken by states, the representation from each state having one vote; a quorum for this purpose shall consist of a member or members from two-thirds of the states, and a majority of all the states shall be necessary to a choice.
[And if the House of Representatives shall not choose a President whenever the right of choice shall devolve upon them, before the fourth day of March next following, then the Vice-President shall act as President, as in case of the death or other constitutional disability of the President. --]* The person having the greatest number of votes as Vice-President, shall be the Vice-President, if such number be a majority of the whole number of Electors appointed, and if no person have a majority, then from the two highest numbers on the list, the Senate shall choose the Vice-President; a quorum for the purpose shall consist of two-thirds of the whole number of Senators, and a majority of the whole number shall be necessary to a choice. But no person constitutionally ineligible to the office of President shall be eligible to that of Vice-President of the United States.

*Later Superseded by section 3 of the 20th amendment.

AMENDMENT XIII
Passed by Congress January 31, 1865. Ratified December 6, 1865.

Note: A portion of Article IV, section 2, of the Constitution was superseded by the 13th amendment.

Section 1.
Neither slavery nor involuntary servitude, except as a punishment for crime whereof the party shall have been duly convicted, shall exist within the United States, or any place subject to their jurisdiction.

Section 2.
Congress shall have power to enforce this article by appropriate legislation.

AMENDMENT XIV
Passed by Congress June 13, 1866. Ratified July 9, 1868.
Note: Article I, section 2, of the Constitution was modified by section 2 of the 14th amendment.

Section 1.
All persons born or naturalized in the United States, and subject to the jurisdiction thereof, are citizens of the United States and of the State wherein they reside. No State shall make or enforce any law which shall abridge the privileges or immunities of citizens of the United States; nor shall any State deprive any person of life, liberty, or property, without due process of law; nor deny to any person within its jurisdiction the equal protection of the laws.

Section 2.
Representatives shall be apportioned among the several States according to their respective numbers, counting the whole number of persons in each State, excluding Indians not taxed. But when the right to vote at any election for the choice of electors for President and Vice-President of the United States, Representatives in Congress, the Executive and Judicial officers of a State, or the members of the Legislature thereof, is denied to any of the male inhabitants of such State, being twenty-one years of age,* and citizens of the United States, or in any way abridged, except for participation in rebellion, or other crime, the basis of representation therein shall be reduced in the proportion which the number of such male citizens shall bear to the whole number of male citizens twenty-one years of age in such State.

Section 3.
No person shall be a Senator or Representative in Congress, or elector of President and Vice-President, or hold any office, civil or military, under the United States, or under any State, who, having previously taken an oath, as a member of Congress, or as an officer of the United States, or as a member of any State legislature, or as an executive or judicial officer of any State, to support the Constitution of the United States, shall have engaged in insurrection or rebellion against the same, or given aid or comfort to the enemies thereof. But Congress may by a vote of two-thirds of each House, remove such disability.

Section 4.
The validity of the public debt of the United States, authorized by law, including debts incurred for payment of pensions and bounties for services in suppressing insurrection or rebellion, shall not be questioned. But neither the United States nor any State shall assume or pay any debt or obligation incurred in aid of insurrection or rebellion against the United States, or any claim for the loss or emancipation of any slave; but all such debts, obligations and claims shall be held illegal and void.

Section 5.
The Congress shall have the power to enforce, by appropriate legislation, the provisions of this article.

*Later Changed by section 1 of the 26th amendment.

AMENDMENT XV
Passed by Congress February 26, 1869. Ratified February 3, 1870.

Section 1.
The right of citizens of the United States to vote shall not be denied or abridged by the United States or by any State on account of race, color, or previous condition of servitude--

Section 2.
The Congress shall have the power to enforce this article by appropriate legislation.

AMENDMENT XVI
Passed by Congress July 2, 1909. Ratified February 3, 1913.
Note: Article I, section 9, of the Constitution was modified by amendment 16.
The Congress shall have power to lay and collect taxes on incomes, from whatever source derived, without apportionment among the several States, and without regard to any census or enumeration.

AMENDMENT XVII
Passed by Congress May 13, 1912. Ratified April 8, 1913.
Note: Article I, section 3, of the Constitution was modified by the 17th amendment.
---The Senate of the United States shall be composed of two Senators from each State, elected by the people thereof, for six years; and each Senator shall have one vote. The electors in each State shall have the qualifications requisite for electors of the most numerous branch of the State legislatures.
---When vacancies happen in the representation of any State in the Senate, the executive authority of such State shall issue writs of election to fill such vacancies: Provided, That the legislature of any State may empower the executive thereof to make temporary appointments until the people fill the vacancies by election as the legislature may direct.
---This amendment shall not be so construed as to affect the election or term of any Senator chosen before it becomes valid as part of the Constitution.

AMENDMENT XVIII
Passed by Congress December 18, 1917. Ratified January 16, 1919. Repealed by amendment 21.

Section 1.
After one year from the ratification of this article the manufacture, sale, or transportation of intoxicating liquors within, the importation thereof into, or the exportation thereof from the United States and all territory subject to the jurisdiction thereof for beverage purposes is hereby prohibited.

Section 2.
The Congress and the several States shall have concurrent power to enforce this article by appropriate legislation.

Section 3.
This article shall be inoperative unless it shall have been ratified as an amendment to the Constitution by the legislatures of the several States, as provided in the Constitution, within seven years from the date of the submission hereof to the States by the Congress.

AMENDMENT XIX
Passed by Congress June 4, 1919. Ratified August 18, 1920.
The right of citizens of the United States to vote shall not be denied or abridged by the United States or by any State on account of sex.
Congress shall have power to enforce this article by appropriate legislation.

AMENDMENT XX
Passed by Congress March 2, 1932. Ratified January 23, 1933.
Note: Article I, section 4, of the Constitution was modified by section 2 of this amendment. In addition, a portion of the 12th amendment was superseded by section 3.

Section 1.
The terms of the President and the Vice President shall end at noon on the 20th day of January, and the terms of Senators and Representatives at noon on the 3d day of January, of the years in which such terms would have ended if this article had not been ratified; and the terms of their successors shall then begin.

Section 2.
The Congress shall assemble at least once in every year, and such meeting shall begin at noon on the 3d day of January, unless they shall by law appoint a different day.

Section 3.
If, at the time fixed for the beginning of the term of the President, the President elect shall have died, the Vice President elect shall become President. If a President shall not have been chosen before the time fixed for the beginning of his term, or if the President elect shall have failed to qualify, then the Vice President elect shall act as President until a President shall have qualified; and the Congress may by law provide for the case wherein neither a President elect nor a Vice President shall have qualified, declaring who shall then act as President, or the manner in which one who is to act shall be selected, and such person shall act accordingly until a President or Vice President shall have qualified.

Section 4
The Congress may by law provide for the case of the death of any of the persons from whom the House of Representatives may choose a President whenever the right of choice shall have devolved upon them, and for the case of the death of any of the persons from whom the Senate may choose a Vice President whenever the right of choice shall have devolved upon them.

Section 5.
Sections 1 and 2 shall take effect on the 15th day of October following the ratification of this article.

Section 6.
This article shall be inoperative unless it shall have been ratified as an amendment to the Constitution by the legislatures of three-fourths of the several States within seven years from the date of its submission.

AMENDMENT XXI
Passed by Congress February 20, 1933. Ratified December 5, 1933.
Section 1.
The eighteenth article of amendment to the Constitution of the United States is hereby repealed.

Section 2.
The transportation or importation into any State, Territory, or Possession of the United States for delivery or use therein of intoxicating liquors, in violation of the laws thereof, is hereby prohibited.

Section 3.

This article shall be inoperative unless it shall have been ratified as an amendment to the Constitution by conventions in the several States, as provided in the Constitution, within seven years from the date of the submission hereof to the States by the Congress.

AMENDMENT XXII
Passed by Congress March 21, 1947. Ratified February 27, 1951.
Section 1.
No person shall be elected to the office of the President more than twice, and no person who has held the office of President, or acted as President, for more than two years of a term to which some other person was elected President shall be elected to the office of President more than once. But this Article shall not apply to any person holding the office of President when this Article was proposed by Congress, and shall not prevent any person who may be holding the office of President, or acting as President, during the term within which this Article becomes operative from holding the office of President or acting as President during the remainder of such term.

Section 2.
This article shall be inoperative unless it shall have been ratified as an amendment to the Constitution by the legislatures of three-fourths of the several States within seven years from the date of its submission to the States by the Congress.

AMENDMENT XXIII
Passed by Congress June 16, 1960. Ratified March 29, 1961.

Section 1.
The District constituting the seat of Government of the United States shall appoint in such manner as Congress may direct:
---A number of electors of President and Vice President equal to the whole number of Senators and Representatives in Congress to which the District would be entitled if it were a State, but in no event more than the least populous State; they shall be in addition to those appointed by the States, but they shall be considered, for the purposes of the election of President and Vice President, to be electors appointed by a State; and they shall meet in the District and perform such duties as provided by the twelfth article of amendment.

Section 2.
The Congress shall have power to enforce this article by appropriate legislation.

AMENDMENT XXIV
Passed by Congress August 27, 1962. Ratified January 23, 1964.
Section 1.
The right of citizens of the United States to vote in any primary or other election for President or Vice President, for electors for President or Vice President, or for Senator or Representative in Congress, shall not be denied or abridged by the United States or any State by reason of failure to pay poll tax or other tax.

Section 2.
The Congress shall have power to enforce this article by appropriate legislation.

AMENDMENT XXV
Passed by Congress July 6, 1965. Ratified February 10, 1967.
Note: Article II, section 1, of the Constitution was affected by the 25th amendment.

Section 1.

In case of the removal of the President from office or of his death or resignation, the Vice President shall become President.

Section 2.
Whenever there is a vacancy in the office of the Vice President, the President shall nominate a Vice President who shall take office upon confirmation by a majority vote of both Houses of Congress.

Section 3.
Whenever the President transmits to the President pro tempore of the Senate and the Speaker of the House of Representatives his written declaration that he is unable to discharge the powers and duties of his office, and until he transmits to them a written declaration to the contrary, such powers and duties shall be discharged by the Vice President as Acting President.

Section 4.
Whenever the Vice President and a majority of either the principal officers of the executive departments or of such other body as Congress may by law provide, transmit to the President pro tempore of the Senate and the Speaker of the House of Representatives their written declaration that the President is unable to discharge the powers and duties of his office, the Vice President shall immediately assume the powers and duties of the office as Acting President.
---Thereafter, when the President transmits to the President pro tempore of the Senate and the Speaker of the House of Representatives his written declaration that no inability exists, he shall resume the powers and duties of his office unless the Vice President and a majority of either the principal officers of the executive department or of such other body as Congress may by law provide, transmit within four days to the President pro tempore of the Senate and the Speaker of the House of Representatives their written declaration that the President is unable to discharge the powers and duties of his office. Thereupon Congress shall decide the issue, assembling within forty-eight hours for that purpose if not in session. If the Congress, within twenty-one days after receipt of the latter written declaration, or, if Congress is not in session, within twenty-one days after Congress is required to assemble, determines by two-thirds vote of both Houses that the President is unable to discharge the powers and duties of his office, the Vice President shall continue to discharge the same as Acting President; otherwise, the President shall resume the powers and duties of his office.

AMENDMENT XXVI
Passed by Congress March 23, 1971. Ratified July 1, 1971.
Note: Amendment 14, section 2, of the Constitution was modified by section 1 of the 26th amendment.

Section 1.
The right of citizens of the United States, who are eighteen years of age or older, to vote shall not be denied or abridged by the United States or by any State on account of age.

Section 2.
The Congress shall have power to enforce this article by appropriate legislation.

AMENDMENT XXVII
Originally proposed Sept. 25, 1789. Ratified May 7, 1992.
No law, varying the compensation for the services of the Senators and Representatives, shall take effect, until an election of representatives shall have intervened.
http://www.archives.gov/national-archives-experience/charters/constitution_amendments_11-27.html

Appendix G Constitutional Amendments Not Ratified

These are the proposed amendments to the Constitution—not ratified by the States.

During the course of our history, in addition to the 27 amendments that have been ratified by the required three-fourths of the States, six other amendments have been submitted to the States but have not been ratified by them.

Beginning with the proposed Eighteenth Amendment, Congress has customarily included a provision requiring ratification within seven years from the time of the submission to the States. The Supreme Court in Coleman v. Miller, 307 U.S. 433 (1939), declared that the question of the reasonableness of the time within which a sufficient number of States must act is a political question to be determined by the Congress.

In 1789, twelve proposed articles of amendment were submitted to the States. Of these, Articles III through XII were ratified and became the first ten amendments to the Constitution, popularly known as the Bill of Rights. In 1992, proposed Article II was ratified and became the 27th amendment to the Constitution. Proposed Article I which was not ratified is as follows:

"Article the first"

"After the first enumeration required by the first article of the Constitution, there shall be one Representative for every thirty thousand, until the number shall amount to one hundred, after which the proportion shall be so regulated by Congress, that there shall be not less than one hundred Representatives, nor less than one Representative for every forty thousand persons, until the number of Representatives shall amount to two hundred; after which the proportion shall be so regulated by Congress, that there shall not be less than two hundred Representatives, nor more than one Representative for every fifty thousand persons."

Thereafter, in the 2d session of the Eleventh Congress, the Congress proposed the following article of amendment to the Constitution relating to acceptance by citizens of the United States of titles of nobility from any foreign government.

The proposed amendment, which was not ratified by three-fourths of the States, is as follows:

Resolved by the Senate and House of Representatives of the United States of America in Congress assembled, two thirds of both houses concurring, That the following section be submitted to the legislatures of the several states, which, when ratified by the legislatures of three fourths of the states, shall be valid and binding, as a part of the constitution of the United States.

> If any citizen of the United States shall accept, claim, receive or retain any title of nobility or honour, or shall, without the consent of Congress, accept and retain any present, pension, office or emolument of any kind whatever, from any emperor, king, prince or foreign power, such person shall cease to be a citizen of the United States, and shall be incapable of holding any office of trust or profit under them, or either of them.

The following amendment to the Constitution relating to slavery was proposed by the 2d session of the Thirty-sixth Congress on March 2, 1861, when it passed the Senate, having previously passed the House on February 28, 1861. It is interesting to note in this connection that this is the only proposed (and not ratified) amendment to the Constitution to have been signed by the President. The President's signature is considered unnecessary because of the constitutional provision that on the concurrence of two-thirds of both Houses of Congress the proposal shall be submitted to the States for ratification.

> Resolved by the Senate and House of Representatives of the United States of America in Congress assembled, That the following article be proposed to the Legislatures of the several States as an amendment to the Constitution of the United States, which, when ratified by three-fourths of said Legislatures, shall be valid, to all intents and purposes, as part of the said Constitution, viz:
>
> **"Article Thirteen**
>
> "No amendment shall be made to the Constitution which will authorize or give to Congress the power to abolish or interfere, within any State, with the domestic institutions thereof, including that of persons held to labor or service by the laws of said State."

A child labor amendment was proposed by the 1st session of the Sixty-eighth Congress on June 2, 1926, when it passed the Senate, having previously passed the House on April 26, 1926. The proposed amendment, which has been ratified by 28 States, to date, is as follows:

Joint Resolution Proposing an Amendment to the Constitution of the United States

> Resolved by the Senate and House of Representatives of the United States of America in Congress assembled (two-thirds of each House concurring therein), That the following article is proposed as an amendment to the Constitution of the United States, which, when ratified by the legislatures of three-fourths of the several States, shall be valid to all intents and purposes as a part of the Constitution:
>
> **"Article—[no number given].**
>
> "Section 1. The Congress shall have power to limit, regulate, and prohibit the labor of persons under eighteen years of age.
>
> "Section 2. The power of the several States is unimpaired by this article except that the operation of State laws shall be suspended to the extent necessary to give effect to legislation enacted by the Congress."

HOUSE JOINT RESOLUTION 208

An amendment relative to equal rights for men and women was proposed by the 2d session of the Ninety-second Congress on March 22, 1972, when it passed the Senate, having previously passed the House on October 12, 1971. The seven-year deadline for ratification of the proposed amendment was extended to June 30, 1982, by the 2d session of the Ninety-fifth Congress. The proposed amendment, which was not ratified by three-fourths of the States by June 30, 1982, is as follows:

Joint Resolution Proposing an Amendment to the Constitution of the United States Relative to Equal Rights for Men and Women

Resolved by the Senate and House of Representatives of the United States of America in Congress assembled (two-thirds of each House concurring therein), That the following article is proposed as an amendment to the Constitution of the United States, which shall be valid to all intents and purposes as part of the Constitution when ratified by the legislatures of three-fourths of the several States within seven years from the date of its submission by the Congress:

"Article—[No number given]

"Section 1. Equality of rights under the law shall not be denied or abridged by the United States or by any State on account of sex.

"Section. 2. The Congress shall have the power to enforce, by appropriate legislation, the provisions of this article.

"Section. 3. This amendment shall take effect two years after the date of ratification."

HOUSE JOINT RESOLUTION 554

An amendment relative to voting rights for the District of Columbia was proposed by the 2d session of the Ninety-fifth Congress on August 22, 1978, when it passed the Senate, having previously passed the House on March 2, 1978. The proposed amendment, which was not ratified by three-fourths of the States within the specified seven-year period, is as follows:

Joint Resolution Proposing an Amendment to the Constitution To Provide for Representation of the District of Columbia in the Congress

Resolved by the Senate and House of Representatives of the United States of America in Congress assembled (two-thirds of each House concurring therein), That the following article is proposed as an amendment to the Constitution of the United States, which shall be valid to all intents and purposes as part of the Constitution when ratified by the legislatures of three-fourths of the several States within seven years from the date of its submission by the Congress:

"Article—[No number given]

"Section 1. For purposes of representation in the Congress, election of the President and Vice President, and article V of this Constitution, the District constituting the seat of government of the United States shall be treated as though it were a State.

"Section. 2. The exercise of the rights and powers conferred under this article shall be by the people of the District constituting the seat of government, and as shall be provided by the Congress.

"Section. 3. The twenty-third article of amendment to the Constitution of the United States is hereby repealed.

"Section. 4. This article shall be inoperative, unless it shall have been ratified as an amendment to the Constitution by the legislatures of three-fourths of the several States within seven years from the date of its submission."

The End of *The Constitution 4 Dummmies!*

Books by Brian W. Kellly
www.letsgopublish.com; Sold at
www.bookhawkers.com
Email info@ letsgopublish.com for specific ordering info. Our titles include the following:

Great Moments in Notre Dame Football The story about the beginning of US football and ND football in the US as well as the great moemnts and great coaches and players ove the years.

Thank You IBM The story of how IBM helped today's technology millionaires and billionaires gain their vast fortunes

WineDiets.Com PresentsThe Wine Diet Learn how to lose weight while having fun. Four specific diets and some great anecdotes fill this book with fun.

Wilkes-Barre, PA; Return to Glory Wilkes-Barre City's return to glory begins with dreams and ideas. Along with plans and actions, this equals leadership.

The Lifetime Guest Plan. This is a plan which if deployed today would immediately solve the problem of 60 million illegal aliens in the United States.

Geoffrey Parsons' Epoch... The Land of Fair Play Better than the original. The greatest re-mastering of the greatest book ever written on American Civics. It was built for all Americans as the best govt. design in the history of the world.

The Bill of Rights 4 Dummmies This is the best book to learn about your rights. Be the first, to have a "Rights Fest" on your block. You will win for sure!

Sol Bloom's Epoch ...Story of the Constitution This work by Sol Bloom was written to commemorate the Sesquicentennial celebration of the Constitution. It has been remastered by Lets Go Publish! – an excellent read!

The Constitution 4 Dummmies This is the best book to learn about the Constitution. Learn all about the fundamental laws of America.

America for Dummmies!
All Americans should read to learn about this great country.

Just Say No to Chris Christie for President!
Discusses the reasons why Chris Christie is a poor choice for US President

The Federalist Papers by Hamilton, Jay, Madison w/ intro by Brian Kelly
Complete unabridged, easier to read version of the original Federalist Papers

Bring On the American Party!
Demonstrates how Americans can be free from Parties of wimps by starting our own national party called the American Party.

Saving America
This how-to book is about saving our country using strong mercantilist principles. These are the same principles that helped the country from its founding.

RRR:
A unique plan for economic recovery and job creation

Kill the EPA
The EPA seems to hate mankind and love nature. They are also making it tough for asthmatics to breathe and for those with malaria to live. It's time they go.

Taxation Without Representation Second Edition
At the time of the Boston Tea Party, there was no representation. Now, there is no representation again but there are "representatives."

Healthcare Accountability
Who should pay for your healthcare? Whose healthcare should you pay for? Is it a lifetime free ride on others or should those once in need of help have to pay it back when their lives improve?

Jobs! Jobs! Jobs!
Where have all the American Jobs gone and how can we get them back?

IBM I Technical Books

The All Everything Operating System:
The story about IBM's finest operating system, its facilities, and how it came to be.

The All-Everything Machine
The story about IBM's finest computer server.

Chip Wars
The story of the ongoing war between Intel and AMD and the upcoming was between Intel and IBM. This book may cause you to buy or sell somebody's stock.

Can the AS/400 Survive IBM?
Exciting book about the AS/400 in an System i5 World.

The IBM i Pocket SQL Guide.
Complete Pocket Guide to SQL as implemented on System i5. A must have for SQL developers new to System i5. It is very compact yet very comprehensive and it is example driven. Written in a part tutorial and part reference style, this book has tons of SQL coding samples, from the simple to the sublime.

The IBM i Pocket Query Guide.
If you have been spending money for years educating your Query users, and you find you are still spending, or you've given up, this book is right for you. This one QuikCourse covers all Query options.

The IBM I Pocket RPG & RPG IV Guide.
Comprehensive RPG & RPGIV Textbook -- Over 900 pages. This is the one RPG book to have if you are not having more than one. All areas of the language covered smartly in a convenient sized book Annotated PowerPoint's available for self-study (extra fee for self-study package)

9780989999995771